CYPRUS

CYPRUS

The Post-Imperial Constitution

Vassilis K. Fouskas
and Alex O. Tackie

PLUTO PRESS
www.plutobooks.com

First published 2009 by Pluto Press
345 Archway Road, London N6 5AA and
175 Fifth Avenue, New York, NY 10010

www.plutobooks.com

Distributed in the United States of America exclusively by
Palgrave Macmillan, a division of St. Martin's Press LLC,
175 Fifth Avenue, New York, NY 10010

British Library Cataloguing in Publication Data
A catalogue record for this book is available from the British Library

ISBN   978 0 7453 2935 2   Paperback

Library of Congress Cataloging in Publication Data applied for

This book is printed on paper suitable for recycling and made from
fully managed and sustained forest sources. Logging, pulping and
manufacturing processes are expected to conform to the
environmental standards of the country of origin. The paper may
contain up to 70 per cent post-consumer waste.

10   9   8   7   6   5   4   3   2   1

Designed and produced for Pluto Press by
Chase Publishing Services Ltd, Sidmouth, England
Typeset from disk by Stanford DTP Services, Northampton, England
Printed and bound in the European Union by
CPI Antony Rowe, Chippenham and Eastbourne

In memoriam

Dervis Ali Kavatzoglou,
member of the Central Committee of AKEL
(Working Peoples Party),

and

Constantine Misiaoulis,
trade unionist of PEO
(Confederation of Cypriot Labour)

dear Cypriot friends
killed on 11 April 1965

Contents

Conclusion   81

Acknowledgements

Some three years ago, during a London summer event on the Cyprus issue, we were approached by the leading group of the London-based human rights NGO, Lobby for Cyprus, asking us to write a short pamphlet on the so-called 'isolation of Turkish Cypriots' – as they put it to us.

We accepted with pleasure, and set to work. But we told Lobby for Cyprus, to their disappointment, that this was not an easy undertaking for two main reasons. First, the issue of Turkish Cypriot 'isolation' is inseparable from a number of other complicated themes on the Cyprus issue; and second, there is no reliable statistical information about the areas where the European *acquis* is suspended, that is, where the Turkish Cypriots and the settlers, as well as other ethnicities, mostly from the Middle East and Eastern Europe, live, work and/or are unemployed or idle. Thus, the project dragged on for a while.

It was Kyriakos Christodoulou, the former coordinator of the human rights NGO, who kindly accepted our objections while putting additional pressure on us to write the pamphlet, giving us a free hand as to how to develop and structure the topic. Despite his heavy work schedule, he managed to supply us with useful research information. We are immeasurably indebted to him for his dedication to the project, and we truly hope that it will meet not only his expectations, but also those of the Lobby for Cyprus as a whole. But there is something more to say here.

We know that Kyriakos is a Greek Cypriot refugee from the little village of Aghios Amvrosios, a victim of the 1974 Turkish military operation on the island. But we also know that Kyriakos's struggle for unfettered independence for Cyprus runs in the same footsteps as those of Dervis Ali Kavatzoglou and Constantine Misiaoulis, the two Cypriots killed by imperial interests and their proxies in Cyprus, and to whom this book is dedicated. Kyriakos is in the same moral league as them.

We are thankful to Evangelos Savva, Consul General of the Cyprus High Commission, London, for his perceptive comments on earlier drafts of this work. The text would have been poorer without his sharp corrections and spot-on remarks. We owe a great debt to our anonymous reviewers, to whom Pluto Press sent our manuscript for review. We did our best to meet their requirements and address their concerns.

We thank the Public Information Office, the Department of Finance and the Civil Registry and Migration Department of the Republic of Cyprus for supplying statistical and other economic data about the state of affairs in the areas of the Republic where the European *acquis* is suspended due to the presence of the Turkish army and security personnel since 1974. We are also obliged to Huseyin Isiksal, PhD student at Keele University, UK, for drawing our attention to the website of the State Planning Organisation (SPO), which contains very useful data about the economy of the same areas. Thanks are also due to the Embassy of the Republic of Cyprus in Athens, particularly to the Ambassador, Professor George Giorghi, and Ms Lida Kapranou from the Press and Information Office.

Our endorsees, whose comments figure on the cover, have read the manuscript, making us think twice about several of the arguments we are putting forward in this work. We did our best to improve the text. We believe that we say something innovative here, and we can only hope that the published version meets their high expectations, as well as those of the reader.

Chronicle of the Cyprus Crisis

This chronicle refers only to the modern era

1571–1878   Ottoman period. Ottoman Porte restores Greek Orthodox Church in parallel with a policy of emigration of Ottoman Muslims to Cyprus. The Greeks were recognised as a 'millet' (nation) under the leadership of their Church and the Archbishop. After 1660, Archbishop becomes 'millet bashi', or Ethnarch.

1878   The beginning of British colonialism in Cyprus. Turkey ceded Cyprus to Britain in return for British help in the Ottoman–Russian war.

1914   Britain officially annexes Cyprus, after Ottoman Turkey sides with the Central Powers in World War I.

1915   Britain offers Cyprus to Greece on condition that Greece enters the war on the side of the allies.

1925   Cyprus becomes a Crown colony, after Turkey renounces (article 16 of Lausanne Treaty of 1923) all her rights over Cyprus.

1931 Anti-colonial and pro-enosis struggles in Nicosia. Government House is burnt down and Constitution suspended. Eleftherios Venizelos, the Greek premier, says in the Greek Parliament that there is no such a thing as a Cypriot problem between Britain and Greece. The problem is between Britain and the Cypriots.

1940s Cypriots promised self-rule and enosis in return for support for the British war effort against Germany. Instead, after the war, they receive – and turn down – a set of constitutional proposals for limited self-rule.

1950 Archbishop Makarios III holds a referendum, which shows 96 per cent of Greek Cypriots in favour of self-determination. Makarios elected Archbishop.

1954 Britain, in defiance of the Treaty of Lausanne, introduces the idea of a tripartite Conference (Greece, Turkey and Britain) to discuss the Cyprus issue. Greece objects but finally accepts. Grivas, an extreme right-winger who fought against the Greek Communists during the Greek Civil War (1944–49) using terrorist methods, arrives secretly in Cyprus to organise the liberation struggle.

1955 EOKA (National Organisation of Cypriot Fighters) anti-colonial campaign begins on 1 April, but the Communist Left does not participate. Tripartite Conference in London begins on 29 August. Riots in Izmir and Istanbul against the Greek minorities.

1956–57 Makarios exiled to the Seychelles. Makarios begins to realise that Grivas's guerrilla campaign cannot lead to enosis, as Britain has openly pitted the Turkish Cypriots against the Greek Cypriots, with the former demanding, taksim (partition). Turkish nationalism in Cyprus boosted. Armed anti-colonial struggle plays straight into the hands of partition.

1958 After the rejection of the Harding and Radcliffe proposals, Macmillan proposes a plan based on the notion of condominium of Cyprus by NATO powers Britain, Turkey and Greece. Denktash, under the direct involvement of Turkey, forms TMT, Turkish Resistance Organisation, fighting for partition.

1959–60 London–Zurich agreements signed. EOKA ceases operation in March. Archbishop Makarios becomes President and Dr Fazil Kütçük Vice-President of the Republic of Cyprus.

1961 Cyprus becomes a member of the Council of Europe.

1963–65 Inter-communal violence breaks out, after Makarios proposes 13 Constitutional amendments that reduce the power of Turkish Cypriots but make the Republic governable. Turkish Cypriot nationalists withdraw into militarily protected enclaves. The British soldiers draw the 'Green Line' in Nicosia between the Greek and Turkish Cypriot quarters. US President Johnson sends letter to Inönü warning that Turkey will not be assisted by the US if Russia moves against her as a response to a Turkish intervention in Cyprus. Greece and Turkey assume new role to solve the Cyprus issue on the basis of Dean Acheson's NATO partition schemes. Makarios finds out about the secret meetings and, together with Andreas Papandreou, blocks the schemes. The Greek premier, George Papandreou, secretly sends a division to Cyprus to overthrow Makarios and pave the way for partition/'double enosis'. In March 1965, UN mediator Galo Plaza produces a balanced report for a solution to the problem, which Turkey rejects out of hand.

1967 Military coup in Greece on 21 April. Most military officers are on the payroll of the CIA. Fighting in Cyprus between Grivas's forces and Turkish Cypriots in Kophinou leads to Turkish ultimatum. Turkey's intervention averted after withdrawal of the Greek division from Cyprus.

1970   Abortive attempt on Makarios's life.

1971–74   Grivas returns secretly to Cyprus and renews campaign for enosis with the formation of EOKA B. Makarios denounces openly and in writing the Greek junta's attempt to eliminate him in order to NATOise and partition Cyprus. Athens Polytechnic events overthrow Papadopoulos's junta bringing into power a more extremist pro-NATO faction under Ioannides. 15 July 1974, coup against Makarios, followed by two full-scale invasions by Turkey (20 July and 14 August). Turkey's forces expand occupation to 37 per cent of Cyprus.

1977–79   High level agreements between Greek and Turkish Cypriot leaders talk of a 'bi-communal federation'. Death of Makarios in 1977.

1983   Unilateral declaration of the 'Turkish Republic of Northern Cyprus'. Turkey gives permission to the US to operate the air base of Incirlik, eastern Turkey.

1990   The Republic of Cyprus applies to join the European Community. France supports the Greek attempt for membership without a solution.

1991   Turkey supports US war against Saddam in Kuwait.

1992   Although turned down, UN Secretary-General Boutros Ghali's 'Set of Ideas' paves the ground for the Annan plan (to arrive ten years later), with notions of confederation.

1996–98   Greco-Turkish crisis in the Aegean over the uninhabited islets of Imia/Kardak. The Republic of Cyprus orders S-300 missiles from Russia. Under threats by Turkey to attack them on arrival, the missiles are placed in Crete.

1999–2004   Beginning of UN-led 'proximity talks' (New York City, 3 December 1999). Face-to-face talks between Clerides and Denktash in Nicosia begin (16 January 2002). Annan submits his first plan on 11 November 2002. Demonstrations of 70,000 Turkish Cypriots in the Turkish Cypriot sector of Nicosia demanding Denktash's resignation (14 January 2003). The Republic of Cyprus signs the EU Treaty of Accession (16 April 2003), which comes into effect on 1 May 2004. Annan's efforts come to an end, after Greek Cypriots vote against a fifth version of the plan (24 April 2004). The EU decides to open accession negotiations with Turkey (17 December).

2005   Talat, a left-winger, wins elections in the areas where the European *acquis* is suspended, renewing hopes for a just and fair settlement for all Cypriots.

2008   AKEL President Christofias wins Presidential vote in the Republic of Cyprus (February) and renews hopes for a solution on the basis of an anti-imperial/anti-nationalist agenda. Talks between Talat and Christofias begin under UN auspices (September).

Introduction

The central idea of this short book is to criticise the imperial arrangements that have governed Cyprus from 1958–60 to date, and propose some sensible steps as to what the Cypriot Left, both Turkish and Greek, can do in order to reach a *post-imperial* constitutional understanding. In this way, we argue, a new era of peaceful inter-faith and inter-ethnic co-existence can start on the island.

The book argues that it is high time now, with the advent to power of two left-wing parties on both sides of the Green Line, to initiate an *anti*-imperial dialogue in order to launch a *post*-imperial constitutional process, immune from great power and NATO engineering. This constitutional process can be initiated, not least because the Republic of Cyprus is a member of the EU, but not a member of NATO. In other words, this long essay is written, quite unashamedly and *mutatis mutandis*, in the spirit of the tradition of Dervis Ali Kavatzoglou and Constantine Misiaoulis, to whom this book is dedicated.

1

Most political histories and treatises on the Cyprus issue suffer from a lack of understanding of the *Cypriot Constitution* and the geo-strategic imperial interests encoded in it. This constitution is not like those that exist in other, let us say 'normal', countries. In a 'normal' country, you have a written or, in the case of Britain, unwritten Constitution, which governs the domestic affairs of the state in a (formally) sovereign manner. But the Cypriot constitution is nothing like that. In effect, it does not exist as a solid and structured body of legal text from which emanate the (formal) powers and obligations of the ruler and the ruled. The Cypriot constitution is an immense body of treaties, laws, agreements and other arrangements which, invariably imposed by outside imperial interference, have been regulating not only the governance of the island from 1960 to date, but also the solution to the Cyprus question as such.

The Cypriot constitution, therefore, is something like the European *acquis*. As such, however, it enjoys a strange 'prerogative'. From the partition plan envisaged by Macmillan's government in 1958 to the Ghali 'Set of Ideas' (1992) and the Annan plan(s) of 2002–04, the solution to the Cyprus issue has in great part been built on constitutional and other arrangements that go against the spirit of international and European law. Cyprus does not even qualify for the euphemism of 'sovereign country'. Yet these arrangements have been signed and/or supported not only by the great transatlantic powers interested in that geo-strategically important part of the world, but also by the leaders of the Cypriot communities themselves. How has that been possible, and what can be done by the Cypriots today to undo this illegal imperial constraint that determines their political future, peaceful co-existence and human security? We attempt to answer this question by way of resorting to an anti-imperial reading of international and domestic politics surrounding Cyprus's post-war history, thus setting out an original research agenda leading to further research questions with a clear and progressive policy orientation. It is an effort that might be relevant, then, not only to the average Cypriot or Cypriot politician, but also to European governments and leaders, simply because a constitutional arrangement reached between the two communities on the island will affect the primary law of the EU.

Imperial Britain in Cyprus has pitted the minority Turks against the majority Greeks in order to obtain clear strategic benefits in and around Cyprus (sovereign base rights, listening posts, intelligence gathering facilities, freedom of military movements in and around the island etc.). Britain's policy of divide and rule, what we prefer to call 'vivisection', fits into the US policy of building garrison-prison states across Eurasia and the Balkans, particularly after the dissolution of the Soviet Union. This 'construct' of garrison-prison state, based on Harold Lasswell's original work in the second part of the 1930s and early 1940s, is applied here to the case of US grand imperial strategy after the Cold War, which aims at an ethnic ghettoisation of Eurasia in order to achieve specific security and class objectives as a global power (protecting trans-national corporations across the globe linked to US interests, guaranteeing the primacy of the dollar in currency markets, safeguarding the transportation of oil and gas to Western markets at stable prices, preventing the emergence of a powerful coalition in Eurasia that could challenge its geo-strategic primacy in the continent etc.). This policy the UN is at pains to endorse (see the example of Kosovo), yet it is a policy which post-Cold War re-emerging powers, such as Russia, are using as an alibi to ascertain their own class and security objectives. Clearly, this is the case of South Ossetia and Abkhazia, which have now qualified for 'garrison-prison' states under Russian protection.

We have opted to build our arguments here *in tandem* with a polemic against a significant number of analyses, which say nothing substantial, or new, about Cyprus. One of the most salient features of these analyses is that they embrace *humbug*. Quite unashamedly, they say so many misleading and historically inaccurate things, as to lead us to become very suspicious about their motives, let alone scholarly standards. We in fact aver that imperial powers have always been in need of intellectuals to embed their policy in society by way of employing a *humbug* discourse, that is, a professionally defined discourse, disinterested in approaching the truth. Although not lies, *humbug* is worse than lies, because it aims at creating a politically subservient subjecthood across the social board, a social subjecthood that accepts imperial rule as the only rule.[1] This is the 'realism' of our 'healthy-minded' neo-liberals and constructivists that we oppose all along. Unfortunately, this discourse seems to have penetrated sections of the Cypriot and European Left. We are aiming at disclosing the inadequacies of this discourse and denounce its – often – spurious scope.

In fact, much of what has been written so far on the Cyprus issue constitutes *humbug*. For instance, this is the discourse that attributes 'equal political rights to the two ethnic communities on Cyprus' in order to build two separate states on the island. This is also true of the discourse on 'lifting the isolation of Turkish Cypriots', against which the Greek Cypriot side has adopted a defensive stance, precisely because it is unable to understand it as *humbug*. It then goes without saying that the intellectual defence of the illegal schemes that aim at legitimising the partitions of Cyprus between

NATO powers Britain, Turkey and Greece can only be based on lies and *humbug*. Yet, a Cypriot *acquis* has been formed since 1957–58 (the Macmillan plan), which is against international and European law. In this context, the way to tackle *humbug* discourse intellectually is to opt out of its cultural zone, something which this short book attempts to establish. We argue that this is the first step Cyprus should take, so that we can start thinking of a Cypriot society and politics *after imperialism*.

The Annan plan was garnished with superb *humbug* discourse of all kinds: academic, journalistic, 'think-tankish', amalgamating the most conspicuous illegalities in terms of international and European law (*acquis communautaire*), hence the extensive set of derogations it included. Politically, the way to tackle *humbug* in this case is to opt out of the security constraints imposed by NATO and Anglo-Saxon power in the eastern Mediterranean. Cypriot society did it first, by voting against the plan. In this context, we also argue that, if the Annan plan had been approved, then the illegal Cypriot *acquis* would have become primary EU law, thus further undermining the EU's (elusive) political and economic cohesion. It is therefore imperative for the EU, we aver, to insist on the implementation of its *acquis* for a Cyprus solution, instead of the one based on the illegal Cypriot *acquis* drawn on accumulated

Anglo-Saxon machinations since 1958. Turkey's interests converge with those of the EU, not least because further securitisation of its soft underbelly, coupled with Middle Eastern contingencies (e.g. the Kurdish issue), may well place it on the perimeter of the *garrison state* policy of the USA, which means possible future vivisection of Turkey, too, on ethnic grounds.

The so-called 'isolation' of Turkish Cypriots can only be analysed and understood within the framework of the regional developmental gap between the northern Cypriot areas where the European *acquis* is suspended (ASA – Areas of Suspended Acquis), and the southern areas under the political control of the Greek Cypriot-led Republic. In practice, from an economic point of view, the issue can be addressed only by encouraging island-wide trade and investment under the aegis of the EU, without excluding simultaneous direct trade and investment with ASA on the proviso that the Republic is involved in it, and that the whole process is viewed in social and not just ethnic-political-separatist terms. But the key issue is island-wide economic cooperation and societal integration.

The Cypriot Left is in office both in ASA and in the Greek Cypriot-led Republic. Relatively untouched by the illegal constitutional engineering of the past and great power machinations, it is high time now for it to insist on a solution based on the principle of opting out of the accumulated illegal Cypriot *acquis*, the product of outdated colonialism and power-politics engineering. For this to be successful, this essay argues, *the next Cyprus plan, the post-imperial plan, should be written by Cypriots themselves.* This is the principle and anything short of this will lead to the dissolution of Cypriot society, more so than its Republic, into a permanent and generalised garrison-prison state of affairs.

This short book is structured around three chapters. The first looks at the ways in which Britain has historically contributed, more than any other actor, including Turkey, to the current state of affairs in Cyprus: an island divided between a Greek Cypriot southern part, which represents the internationally recognised government on the island, and the Turkish Cypriot part, where the European *acquis* is suspended (Turkey has maintained there a nearly 40,000 strong army and security personnel since 1974). In that chapter, we also define '*humbug*' and come to grips with samples of *humbug* discourse pertaining to the case of Cyprus. The second chapter examines the post-1974 historical period and substantiates further the strategic importance of the island for NATO's imperial interests. This chapter also lays down the defining characteristics of the concept of the 'garrison-prison state', as it was first developed by sociologist Harold

Lasswell. The final chapter, inspired by Mehmet Ugur's pioneering work on the Cypriot developmental gap between the North and the South, examines in some detail the structured income and per capita inequalities between Greek and Turkish Cypriots, and provides some policy alternatives about how to bridge the already diminishing inequality between the average Greek and Turkish Cypriot.

1
Narrating Cyprus

BEYOND HUMBUG

The Cyprus issue, in one way or another, has always preoccupied imperial European politics. From 1878, when the island was leased to Britain by the Ottoman Turks, to the British suggestions for handing it over to Greece in order to cajole it to enter World War I on the side of the allies, and from the Cypriot uprisings of 1931 and the 1950s for union with Greece to the entry into the EU and the UN-sponsored plan(s) of 2002–04, Cyprus has been on the agenda of European politics, played out on Eurasia's grand plateau.

But if the 'Eastern Question' and the 'Great Game' – these horrific imperial attempts by the British, the Russians, the Italians and the French to dissolve the Ottoman Empire and vivisect the Arab Middle East and Muslim Central Asia between them – have inserted Cyprus into the 'European family', that very fact has at the same time, by location, default and design, made it a pawn in the strategic calculations of the West's Middle Eastern and Central Asian policies. In this respect, for over a century now, domestic Cypriot politics and ethnic/religious relations have been manipulated by the imperial West to such an outrageous and derogatory extent, as to defy the intellectual honesty and dignity of the researcher, particularly when dealing with primary sources on the Cyprus issue. The greatest achievement of the West in Cyprus over the last one hundred years – inclusive of the USA at least since 1963 – has been that it has managed to simultaneously *re-define* and *divide* two peoples on one relatively small island, the majority Greek Cypriots (80 per cent) and the minority Muslims (18 per cent) – the remaining 2 per cent being Maronites and Armenians – turning them into Greek and Turkish nationalists fighting each other. The process of *re-definition*, it should be noted, has taken place *pari passu* with that of *division*. The Greek Cypriot had to be re-defined as an anti-Turk nationalist, and the Muslim Cypriot as a pro-Turkish, anti-Greek nationalist.

Imperial powers and their proxies tend to ask the wrong questions publicly, almost always on purpose. They ask the wrong questions, because they are unconcerned with the true–false nature of their statement of facts. Instead, Harry G. Frankfurt says, they do so because they want to *bullshit*. *Bullshit* aims at misrepresenting the nature or intentions of the bullshitter using artful screens of language. 'Because *bullshit* is unconcerned with the truth', Frankfurt continues, '*bullshit* is a greater enemy of the truth than lies are.'[2] A liar's craft is bound to the world of true facts, because the lie must replace a truth. *Bullshitting* is the greatest enemy of scholarship, because it creates an image of fact without producing any in the form of concrete historical evidence. Yet it has the advantage of being perceived by the reader or the spectator as having a permanent and solid cognitive and factual value. At times, *humbug* discourse artfully employs 'duplicity', 'dubiousness' and 'ambivalence', simply because it is indifferent to how things really are. By declaring its wish to 'satisfy both parties', *bullshit* turns out to serve the interests of the social/political class and the state it serves.

What happens if people in Cyprus do not wish to live together, asks a report produced by the International Crisis Group:

Greek Cypriots portray the island's history as Hellenic, ethnically and culturally Greek, and put aside other narratives and the island's subjection to many overlords. Turkish Cypriots claim an equal share of the history on the basis of many centuries of residence, as well as the legacy and monuments of

307 years of Ottoman Turkish rule, one of the longest periods the island spent under a single master.[3]

The ICG report of 27 pages and 200 footnotes, of which 190 are interviews with 'Turkish' and 'Greek' officials, 'academics', 'researchers' and 'peace activists', falls within Frankfurt's epistemological-analytical definition of *bullshit*.

Similarly, an older report prepared by the Centre for European Policy Studies in Brussels (CEPS) tells us that for the Cyprus problem to be solved, 'there is a need for an adequate *exit from conflict model*' (emphasis in the original), primarily because it is the Cypriots that should be blamed for the current situation of division and tension. And then the same report goes on to suggest a 'consociational' solution to the plight of the island through its own definition of Europe, because, after all, 'the EU itself is somewhat federal, somewhat co-federal and somewhat *sui generis*'.[4] A Cyprus solution, then, can draw from a combination of all these three features of the EU.

Western hegemonic officialdom, having redefined the narrative of the Cyprus issue alongside its vivisections, is now arguing that, inasmuch as there are two ethnically and religiously defined communities on the island, a co-federal, that is a two-state, solution is the only one to settle the problem this very officialdom created.

'Both sides share responsibility for the outcome [of the 1974 Turkish invasions]', says Fred Halliday, blaming Ecevit, the Turkish premier who ordered the Turkish troops to invade, because he 'interrupted his breakfast' – the LSE Professor was on holiday in Cyprus at the time.[5] Ecevit, of course, cracked a smile at Halliday's comment (they had both met at a Chatham House event after the invasion and Halliday had the chance to air his complaint).

Liars love *humbug*. It snugly gives an ending to their story. Turkish nationalists on Cyprus happily embrace *humbug* analytical perspectives, in fact a political donation to them: 'There is not, and there has never been, a Cypriot nation' are the opening lines of Rauf Denktash's book on Cyprus, first published in 1982.[6] There are Turks and Greeks both wanting self-determination. And because of the Greeks' campaign of terror from 1960 to 1974, Turkey intervened to create a safe heaven for the Turks of Cyprus. The international community, however, wrongly supported the Greeks by not recognising the Turkish Cypriot state. Thus, 'the isolation of Turkish Cypriots should be lifted', especially today, because they voted in favour of the UN blueprint for the 'reunification' of the island in 2004 – the so-called 'Annan plan' – after the name of the then UN Secretary-General, Kofi Annan.[7] Note how lies end in *humbug*: as we shall see, the entire discourse that pertains to the framework of the UN's most recent blueprint was not about re-unification of Cyprus, but legitimisation of a garrison-prison state of affairs on the island, in contrast to the rest of the EU.

Yet, the answer to issues such as 'there is no Cypriot nation', or 'what happens if the Greek and the Turkish Cypriots cannot live together', is that *these questions are non-starters*. The same goes for the *humbug* discourse of 'the isolation of Turkish Cypriots', as well as other stories. If wrong questions are asked publicly, then wrong answers are produced publicly. Yet, because this is bordering on *bullshit*, and the great powers and their intellectuals know that, they also know both the right questions and the right answers *in private*. This is exactly the aim of this essay: to decipher and re-contextualise, as much as possible and practicable, the right questions and the right answers, which are deliberately hidden by the West's imperial discourse.

MAKARIOS BETRAYED

The situation on the island today is primarily, that is to say historically, the result of Britain's strategic planning in the 1950s and early 1960s, aiming at dividing the island between Greek and Turkish sectors, while keeping for itself some big chunks of land to use as military bases, building intelligence gathering and logistical support facilities for operations in the Middle East and the Caucasus/Central Asia. Britain, facing the Greek Cypriots' ferocious anti-colonial uprising, pitted the Turks against the Greeks by way of setting up auxiliary police units totally composed of Turkish Cypriots. Turkish Cypriots, recruited from the poorest and most uneducated Cypriot social strata, tortured Greek Cypriots under the blissful eye of British lieutenants. At the political level, and contrary to the provisions of article 16 of the Lausanne Treaty (1923), which still, seemingly, regulates Greek–Turkish relations, Britain invited Turkey, on an equal footing with Greece, to participate in tri-partite diplomatic talks, thus making Turkey a party to the Cyprus issue.[8] Note that well into 1957, that is more than two years after the beginning of the EOKA guerrilla campaign (National Organisation of Cypriot Fighters) for self-determination and union with Greece, EOKA fighters did not have any political objective against their Turkish Cypriot compatriots, strictly considering and acting upon orders pertaining to the ousting of British rule from the island.[9] It was Britain who encouraged and sponsored the development of Turkish Cypriot nationalism on the island, both directly and via Turkey, thus reawakening a Muslim community whose contacts with the European Enlightenment and the tradition of nationalism were until the early 1950s minimal.[10] Had Britain refused to stir up conflict between Greek Cypriots and Muslims/ Turkish Cypriots, the ethnic definition of the Muslim at a mass level might have evolved in a number of ways, the likelihood being that only a minority elite of Muslims would have espoused Turkish nationalism. In this respect, the construction and definition of Turkish Cypriot nationalism as a mass movement on the island is primarily the work of British imperialism, rather than of local enlightened Turkish Cypriot elites acting under European-nationalist influences – as was the case, for example, with other Balkan nationalisms, including Greek and Greek Cypriot nationalism. Britain, notes Perry Anderson in his intellectual *tour de force* on the Cyprus issue, could have allowed self-determination to take place, following the example of the Italians in Rhodes and the Dodecanese complex of islands in the 1940s, which also had a Muslim/Turkish minority. But Britain was not Italy, and Britain's record of 'divide and rule', from Ireland to Kashmir, is bad enough not to need further certificates.[11]

The birth of the Republic of Cyprus in 1960 was as truncated as the political will of Greece to stand up to Britain's imperial policy.[12] When Makarios, the charismatic leader of Cyprus with much sympathetic support, even among Turkish Cypriots and Muslims, asked Karamanlis in Athens to block the implementation of the British plan – inspired by Macmillan – for the division of Cyprus by threatening to withdraw Greece from NATO if it went ahead, Karamanlis refused even to entertain it as a thought. It was then that Makarios came out loudly in favour of independence, shelving *enosis* (union with Greece) – nobody knowing for how long. Independence he got, but even this was truncated.

On two other encounters of great importance with the Conservative Greek government in Zürich and London, this time before he signed the constitutional agreements of 1959–60, Makarios's political vision was severely twisted by the Greek premier and his foreign minister, Averof, the result being an unworkable constitution, the aim of which was more to guarantee the colonial interests of Britain than the functionality of the central government of the Republic. Characteristically, a US State Department Report at the time had criticised the cumbersome nature of the settlements and predicted their collapse.[13]

Capitalising on the right to veto decisions on foreign and economic matters, the Turkish Cypriot Vice Presidency of the Republic, in conformity with Britain's partition policy, abused this right, thus making the Cypriot polity virtually ungovernable. Frictions also arose on the questions of separate municipalities, the formation of a Cypriot army, the implementation of the 70:30 ratio in the staffing of the state machine etc.[14] As pointed out in the State Department Report and by Makarios, the constitution was a recipe for division, not cooperation, depriving an ethnic majority of the means to democratically manage an ethnic minority. That is how the Cyprus issue can be defined from 1960 down to 1974.

The British partition policy on Cyprus was upheld by the Turkish Cypriot leadership and Turkey itself, and was additionally endorsed by Acheson's and Ball's conspiracy plans of 1964–65.[15] It could also be argued that the faction of Greek Cypriot nationalists who gathered around General Grivas, the leader of the military arm of EOKA, played straight into the hands of the advocates of partition, since it aroused Turkish Cypriot nationalism further. Grivas might have been fighting for *enosis* but, to all intents and purposes, he and his fellow Greek nationalists, or some of them, were working – whether wittingly or unwittingly we are not in a position to know – for the undercurrents of partition, serving NATO's policy. This is how one could explain the silence of Rauf Denktash about Grivas's military action against Turkish Cypriots: in the event, Grivas was not Denktash's real enemy. The real enemy was Makarios, who became the target of Denktash's narrative throughout (we discuss Denktash's rationale below).

In this context, scholarship should not fail to distinguish the visionary and democratic policy of President Makarios who, in the most extraordinary and adverse circumstances, with his life constantly under threat by Greek extremists and the Greek junta – in power from 1967 to 1974 – wanting a NATO partition plan implemented in Cyprus, envisaged and worked for an independent, democratic and non-aligned Cypriot Republic. And Denktash knew that had Makarios's policy won, it would have been bad news for Turkey's security interests in the Eastern Mediterranean, although not necessarily for NATO and the US as a whole, which could have turned to NATO member Greece for further services, thus damaging Turkey. After all, having two Hellenic states in the Eastern Mediterranean was bad news for Turkish nationalism – period. But matters were not always under Makarios's control.

Inter-communal fights broke in 1963–64 and 1967. In the first instance, in particular, the reason for the fighting was the proposed constitutional amendments put forward by Makarios with Britain's blessing. Makarios, unable to govern due to the constant impediments his policies were encountering from the Turkish Cypriot Vice Presidency, felt it necessary to propose 13 amendments to the constitution. This gave the golden opportunity to the Turkish Cypriot leadership to leave their government positions and parliament, withdrawing into militarily protected enclaves. The entire Turkish Cypriot population was then encouraged to follow them, aiming to create *de facto* social and economic conditions for a permanent partition. Christians and Muslims had been living side by side in mixed villages and towns all over Cyprus for centuries. Understandably enough, the problem for the British and, consequently, for Turkey, was how to unmingle them. But it was then that Makarios's greatest victory came along, namely UN resolution 186, which established a UN peacekeeping force in Cyprus, and which recognised only the legitimate government.

UN SECURITY COUNCIL RESOLUTION 186, AND AFTER

'UN:US' wrote Peter Gowan, the best international relations expert sitting on the editorial board of *New Left Review*.[16] The UN came into being to fulfil Franklin Delano Roosevelt's (FDR) desire for the USA to rule the world via the UN Security Council (UN SC), which in 1944 was composed of Britain, China (not that of Mao, but of the demoralising Kuomintang), the US and USSR ('the four policemen', as FDR put it). France was later brought in, but FDR's plan did not prove so successful, since China turned Communist in 1949, whereas France had become a rather difficult ally to manage. FDR's plan for the UN SC was to enable it to carry out policies in a manner that would have led to the global isolation and defeat of the USSR. But FDR's UN scheme for global domination of the USA moved into the background. The USA's global neo-imperial thinking was now dominated by stars such as Kennan and Acheson, with their theories of containment and 'hub and spoke' notions of global governance.[17] This, however, did not mean that the UN was abandoned as a US policy instrument in the struggle for global supremacy. The UN was and remains as American in policy and scope as Dumbarton Oaks in Georgetown itself, where it was first seriously conceived and all the big decisions were taken.

Yet, in the 1950s and 1960s, the UN as a whole was seen by the USA as a global vehicle of secondary importance. The rise of Arab nationalism, the powerful posture of the USSR, the success of anti-colonial movements and the shift to the Left in Latin America and other parts of the world, made it difficult for the USA to openly manipulate the UN, particularly its General Assembly. Matters of primary importance were delegated to other international and internationalised agencies, whereas issues such as the Greek–Turkish conflict over Cyprus were pushed to behind-the-scenes diplomacy (the backstage), such as the Acheson–Ball conspiracy plan to forcibly vivisect Cyprus between

Greece and Turkey on the basis of a NATO scheme. On the frontstage, that is first and foremost the UN, matters could be regulated via the balance of preferences within its General Assembly – where the overwhelming majority supported Makarios's non-aligned stance – and the SC.

UN-SC Resolution 186 must be seen within this qualified political context. The greatest victory for Makarios, the one that came in the wake of the withdrawal of the Turkish Cypriots into military enclaves in 1963–64 – reinforced by Turkish mainland forces – still represents a political fact of enormous significance for the present and future of a united and independent Cyprus. It is mainly on the basis of this Resolution that subsequent Greek Cypriot leaderships have since been drawing to argue for the existence and continuation of 'their Republic of Cyprus' (note that Turkey, since 1963, has been refusing to recognise the existence of the Republic of Cyprus and its government). That 'Republic' is basically Makarios's own construct, the product of his genius and masterful political manoeuvring in Cold War conditions. Moreover, and despite the pressure to which he was subjected by NATO powers, including Greece, Makarios managed to keep the Cyprus issue outside a NATO framework: for him, quite rightly, such a solution framework entailed partition.

The Resolution, produced on 4 March 1964, recalls article 2, paragraph 4 of the UN Charter, which states that 'all members [of the UN] shall refrain in their international relations from the threat or use of force against the territorial integrity or political independence of any State, or in any other manner inconsistent with the Purposes of the UN'. It then went on to recommend the creation, 'with the consent of the Government of Cyprus', of a United Nations peace-keeping force in Cyprus, the composition and size of which 'shall be established by the Secretary-General, in consultation with the Governments of Cyprus, Greece, Turkey and the United Kingdom of Great Britain and Northern Ireland'. Yet the most important aspect of the Resolution was its very first article which, after the inter-communal fights in 1963–64 and the abandoning by the Turkish Cypriots of their government positions, affirms and recognises as the only legitimate government on the island that led by Makarios: '[The Security Council] *Asks* the Government of Cyprus, which has the responsibility for the maintenance of law and order, to take all additional measures necessary to stop violence and bloodshed in Cyprus'.[18]

The partition of Cyprus between Greece, Turkey and Britain, initiated by the British in the 1950s and enshrined in the constitutional arrangements of 1959–60, were virtually put into practice in 1963–64 with the self-imposed policy of enclaves by the Turkish Cypriots, a policy of which Resolution 186 disapproved. Thus, Turkey's two consecutive advances on Cyprus in summer 1974, came to deepen partition and enlarge Turkey's zone of control whilst violating the Treaty of Guarantee – which allows intervention by the guarantor powers, Britain, Turkey and Greece, on the proviso that it will restore the *status quo ante*. It was, however, the spirit of Resolution 186 that led the Security Council to denounce the Turkish advances as illegal, as well as all subsequent acts of Turkey on the island, such as the creation of a 'Turkish Republic of Northern Cyprus' in 1983. It is no accident that SC Resolution 353 of 20 July 1974, drafted on the very same day of Turkey's first invasion, recalls Resolution 186 and all subsequent Resolutions on this matter, calling 'all States to respect the sovereignty, independence and territorial integrity of Cyprus'. And as if this was not enough bad news for Britain and Turkey, the UN, via its mediator Galo Plaza, produced in 1965 a Report reinforcing Makarios's vision for an independent Cyprus on the basis of majoritarian-democratic rule.

But Makarios's victory was soon to be followed by the tempest of Acheson's and Ball's conspiracy schemes. Acheson, the architect of US post-war grand strategy and now entrusted with solving one of NATO's thorniest problems, conceived of several plans on the

basis of which Cyprus could be partitioned between
the two NATO allies, Greece and Turkey. To Greece,
his philosophy was sold as *enosis*, and that was how its
politicians should deliver it to their public. To Turkey,
this was sold as *taksim* (partition), and that was how its
politicians could deliver it to their public. But for this
to be achieved, Makarios should become, by whatever
means, a spent force. Thus, the Greek government of
George Papandreou sent a division to the island, whose
basic aim was to achieve 'regime change' – to topple
Makarios. With this effected, then the arrangement
between Greece and Turkey allocating to Turkey an
area on Cyprus where it could have had its military
base and other civilian zones of control, including
some Greek territory proper, could have been put into
practice according to the preconceived plan.

All this was happening behind Makarios's back, but
he found out about the conspiracy. He and Andreas
Papandreou, George's talented son in his Centrist
Democratic cabinet and obvious successor to the party
leadership, opposed Acheson's schemes. Acheson also
collided head-on with certain conservative views of
the Turkish generals, who disagreed as to the size of
the zone allocated to Turkish interests. At any event,
Acheson's mission collapsed and the Greek division
withdrew in 1967 when Turkey threatened, for the
second time since 1964, to invade the island.

Importantly, though, the calmest period in Cyprus was that between 1967 and 1974 – the years of the reign of the Greek junta. A solution was, indeed, almost found on the eve of the first invasion, when Greek and Turkish jurists managed to strike a deal not far from the spirit of the proposed Constitutional amendments of Makarios in 1963.[19]

The Turkish invasions of 1974 further deepened the partitions of 1963. They created two contiguous and totally separate ethnic and religious zones, the northern and the southern. Greek Cypriots, Turkish Cypriots, Christians and Muslims, were unmingled totally, for the first time in their modern history. In essence, the events of 1974 – first the Greek junta led by Ioannides toppled Makarios by using the Cypriot National Guard and then Ecevit invaded five days later – were an amateurish implementation of Acheson's conspiracy scheme. Clerides recalls in his memoirs:

> Bluntly, the real objective of the [Greek] conspirators was to oust Makarios and his government in order to proceed with direct negotiations with Turkey, and with the use of the good offices of the United States, to achieve Enosis of the major part of Cyprus with Greece, conceding a smaller part of Cyprus to Turkish sovereignty. At no time did the Greek junta have it in mind to declare Enosis unilaterally and to accept the risk of having military conflict with Turkey.[20]

Denktash, the opposite number of the Greek nationalist
Grivas, who died early in 1974, before the Turkish
intervention, boasted that Greeks and Turks could
live in peace only if separated – look, for instance,
how great the Lausanne Treaty has been with its
forceful population exchange, uprooting hundreds
of thousands of people on both sides. The Turkish
socialist premier at the time of the invasion, Ecevit, and
the USA Secretary of State, Kissinger, whom Hitchens
wanted to sue for crimes against humanity, were happy
with this statement.[21] 'The Cyprus issue was solved in
1974', has been both Ecevit's and Kissinger's argument
ever since. Thus, eventually, it was the Turkish army
that brought the British-inspired policy of partition
to fruition, not any ill-conceived conspiratorial plan
or constitutional engineering. Imperial powers have
always used proxies in history in order to achieve
their aims, disregarding both human suffering and
international law. British policy on the island has been
and remains that of maintaining military bases and
listening posts and other rights in and around Cyprus,
thus supporting its military operations, communication
lines and general security policy in the Near and Middle
East, regions rich in oil, gas and other hydrocarbon
resources. But in achieving these goals Britain has had,
first, to keep the Greeks and the Turks on the island
apart; second, to lend its support to the largest and

most strategically placed country of the dispute that it created, Turkey. Then, last on the list, comes Greece. So it was in the past, and so it remains today with, of course, the added factor of endorsing its Big Brother, the USA, since at least 1963. The vivisection of Cyprus got truly embedded there in 1974.

2

The Partitions of Cyprus after 1974

INTERESTING THOUGHTS

Almost any Cyprus crisis, or grand political design related to a 'solution' of the Cyprus issue in the past, ran in parallel with a critical situation in the Middle East. So it was in 1955–57, with the Suez Canal crisis and the EOKA anti-colonial struggle (note that in 1958 we had the formation of the first secret Turkish–Israeli joint defence understanding). So it was in 1967, with the 'Six Day War', when Israel smashed Arab power, while on Cyprus, the Greek junta was forced to withdraw its division following threats by Turkey to invade the island. The Turkish advances on Cyprus in summer 1974 took place nine months after the Yom Kippur War. The list is indeed long. The proclamation of the 'Turkish Republic of Northern Cyprus' in 1983 was followed by UN-sponsored talks on the Cyprus issue with the participation of Richard Perle, whose aim was to lift a Congress ban on Turkey's financial aid and guarantee the opening and functioning of the US airbase in Diyarbakir, south-east Turkey.[22] The so-called 'Ghali Set of Ideas' of 1992 came in the wake of the first Gulf War and just before the 'Oslo accords', whereas the Annan plan arrived amidst the second Gulf crisis. One of us has tried to expand on these – perhaps coincidental, perhaps not so coincidental – 'parallel stories' elsewhere, by looking into the concrete evidence and archival material available.[23] Whatever the case and the legitimate assumptions one could draw from these parallels in light of concrete evidence, one thing is certain: Cyprus, geo-strategically, belongs to the West's security and defence planning vis-à-vis the Near and Middle East and is thus integrated into political schemes of action that are bound to affect the island each time there is a pronounced crisis or an important 'peace process' in the greater Middle East. So Cyprus is not only 'Europe', with all of the different meanings that it has acquired over the past four centuries, but also the Middle/Near East. As such, it is a useful pawn and bargaining tool both for the imperial and the regional powers in their attempts to defend and/or advance their national-security and class interests.

But what is even more interesting given the perspective through which we are approaching the issues here, is to see how Cyprus is located in, and affected by, the contemporary strategic and security settings of an expanding EU, an expanding NATO and the contingency of the post-9/11 Anglo-Saxon policy in the greater Middle East. We shall see that the Annan plan was indeed the result of a delicate balance of power game – although not so 'powerful' on the part of the EU – unfolding between the EU/France, on the one hand, and the USA–UK/NATO on the other, with Turkey being the bastion of NATO interests in the Near East, and thus the chief regional beneficiary on Cyprus. The UN, in this respect, as well as all the obscure scriveners and advisers who attempted to legitimise the divisions of Cyprus between 2002 and 2004, pushed as much for the appearance of legitimacy, as for their self-congratulating 'mission of good offices in Cyprus'. The Annan plan would not have 'solved' the Cyprus problem had the Greek Cypriots voted for it; it would have simply 'fixed' it and turned it into a garrison-prison state of affairs, so as to enable it to be manipulated by all of its powerful scriveners in the future. This is the context, we shall argue, within which the discourse about the 'isolation of Turkish Cypriots', after the Greek Cypriot rejection of the plan, should be analysed and understood.

THE WEAKENING POSTURE OF
THE REPUBLIC OF CYPRUS IN THE UN

Interestingly, both Greece and Turkey refused to enforce annexation of the territories divided by the force of Turkish arms. It is in this respect, too, that the Acheson conspiracy scheme, implemented in retrospect, should be seen as a failure. The UN bypassed Turkey's excuse for the invasion – 'an intervention in order to protect the Turkish Cypriot minority from Greek aggression and stop union of the island with Greece' – and denounced Turkey's action as illegal, asking for a restoration of the *status quo ante* as per the Treaty of Guarantee of 1959–60. It seemed as if the Turkish occupied sector (37 per cent of the total territory of the island) would remain in a state of civil limbo pending annexation, used in the meantime by Turkey for military purposes alone, as Kissinger boasted in his memoirs, *The Years of Renewal* (1999). It turned out not to be so: Turkish Cypriot society is far more vibrant and modernistic than its masters want us to believe.

Waves of Turkish settlers and unskilled labourers poured into the island's northern security sector, at times directly encouraged by the Turkish government in order to balance the Greek Cypriot demographic advantage. The so-called 'high level agreements' of

1977 between Makarios and Denktash talked about a just and viable solution to the Cyprus problem on the basis of a 'bi-communal federation'. But in 1983, the Turkish Cypriot elite, with the agreement of the Turkish military and the USA, went ahead and unilaterally proclaimed an independent 'Turkish Republic of Northern Cyprus' (TRNC), which was immediately denounced by the UN and the European authorities and which to date has been recognised only by Turkey (this came to replace the 'Turkish Federated State of Northern Cyprus', proclaimed on 13 February 1975, which was also denounced by the UN). However, the defeat of Arab nationalism in the 1970s, coupled with the weakening international position of the USSR in the 1980s, deprived the Greek-led Cyprus of a balancing act in the UN similar to that of the 1960s. More to the point, the creation of a *fait accompli* by Turkey on the ground strengthened the Turkish position, hence its negotiating power, for a Cyprus compromise.

Understandably enough, Greek and Greek Cypriot strategy embraced a pro-European institutional perspective. As the process of European integration was gathering pace with Delors' Single European Act (1986) and the Maastricht Treaty (negotiated and approved during the Yugoslav crisis of 1990–92), the Hellenic bloc in the Eastern Mediterranean saw in the EC/EU a distinctive pole of support for its cause. In May

1987, to Turkish fury, the Republic of Cyprus signed a customs union with the European Communities and in July 1990 submitted its formal application to join them. The objective of Hellenism was entry of the Republic within the EC/EU 'regardless of whether a solution to the problem of the division is found beforehand' via the UN process. At the European Council meeting in Corfu in 1993, when Greece was holding the EU's rotating presidency, the EC took a further step, putting on an equal footing the membership of the Republic with that of East-Central European states. This alarmed the USA and Turkey, but they were both somewhat mollified soon after that, as a customs union agreement between Turkey and the European Communities began to loom large. In a masterly deal crafted under the auspices of France (February–March 1995), the EC went much further and declared that entry negotiations with Cyprus could commence six months after the Amsterdam Inter-Governmental Conference of 1996–97. At the same time, Turkey signed a customs union agreement with the EU. But Turkey was again rebuffed by the EU at the Luxembourg summit of 12–14 December 1997, when a determined Germany stood its ground by not offering Turkey candidate status, despite strong USA pressure. Cyprus's application, however, went ahead, and in April 1998 it formally opened accession negotiations over the *acquis*. A month earlier, the Greek

Cypriot President of the Republic, Glafkos Clerides, had officially asked the Turkish Cypriot leadership to join the Cyprus accession negotiating team, but the Turkish side refused to do so.[24] At the EU's summit of June 1998, the Turkish foreign minister, Mesut Yilmaz had 'a sharp exchange of words with German Foreign Minister Klaus Kinkel', asserting that 'Germany's EU strategy in Central and Eastern Europe was merely a continuation of its Nazi-era *lebensraum* policies'.[25] It was only at the Helsinki summit in December 1999 that Turkey was, grudgingly, offered candidate status, without nevertheless any commitment on the part of Europeans about when to begin accession negotiations. The EU, it should be noted, had set up a committee whose task was to monitor Turkey's progress in fulfilling the Copenhagen criteria and harmonise the country with the *acquis*. This, as well as talk by Europe's conservative circles for a special partnership agreement and not full membership, did not go down well in Turkey, which eventually managed to begin a precarious process over the discussion of the *acquis* in October 2005 – agreed in December 2004. 'Precarious' it is, and not simply because of the Cyprus issue, which the great powers, whether European or not, are constantly using in order either to boost the Turkish national interest, or simply to contain and even damage it. Also precarious because of Turkey's involvement in the Iraqi crisis, not to mention its so-called 'bad human rights record' that the West (the EU and USA), recalls at any time that they see fit.

Meanwhile, the struggle within the UN had continued unabated. It was as if the 'good offices' mission of the Secretary-General – established in the form of the appointment of a mediator in SC Resolution 186 – had to prove itself at all times. And as Hellenism was scoring well against Turkey in the theatre of European institutions, the UN, under the domineering influence of the US, was in a position to shift the boundaries of discussion over Cyprus into a NATO, pro-Anglo-Saxon framework. In November 1984, UN Secretary-General Pérez de Cuéllar drafted a 'framework agreement', calling for a 'bi-zonal Republic', two houses, with a 'senate with equal Greek Cypriot and Turkish Cypriot representation', thus inserting the principle of equality at the federal level.[26] As the first post-Cold War crises in the Persian Gulf and the Balkans were making headlines all over the world, the March 1990 SC Resolution 649 was asking the Greek Cypriot leadership to accept further concessions and go beyond the bi-communal concept of 1977. Giving comfort to *bullshitters*, it defined the Cyprus problem as an 'inter-communal affair' that had to be solved between the two communities on an 'equal basis'. Moreover, 'it defined the parameters of the settlement, but remained silent on the issues of the implementation of UN resolutions, the withdrawal of Turkish forces and the Turkish settlers, the return of the refugees, the three freedoms etc.'.[27] This resolution was followed by Resolution 716 (1991), which was similar in tone and spirit. These initiatives culminated in the April 1992 'Set of Ideas' by Boutros Boutros Ghali.[28] It is important here to note that the report by the Secretary-General, was devastating for the Greek Cypriot side, since it established the principle of 'political equality between the two communities'. It even included a clause, expanding the Turkish Cypriot veto to include the question of membership of the European Communities. This was because of the fear that the Greek-led Republic might join the EC before a solution was found. And with the Republic of Cyprus as a member, Turkey's own accession process would be at stake. However, because of France's objections that such a clause interfered with the powers of the Community, SC Resolution 750 (1992) did not endorse that specific clause of Ghali's 'Set of Ideas'. Yet almost all subsequent UN SC Resolutions from 1990 presented the Cyprus issue as 'an inter-communal affair of two politically equal communities'. The 'good offices' mission of the UN Secretary-General and its Cyprus envoys were setting the stage for what was yet to come.

A GARRISON STATE ENDORSED BY THE UN

The violent dissolution of Yugoslavia laid out new tasks for Western intellectuals to explore: how to revise aspects of international law to make sense of the profiteering business of 'humanitarian intervention' – the Kosovo case being the workshop and starting point for this intellectual exercise; how to explain the proliferation of state-centric ethnic ghettos, at times bound within a supposedly united state, such as the Bosnian one, in the era of globalisation; how to show, in as fashionable a 'liberal' and 'democratic' manner as possible, the way in which co-federal settlements, such as those of Switzerland and Belgium, not to mention the 'Good Friday' agreements over the fate of Northern Ireland, could work in regions and parts of the world with completely different histories, cultures and social norms.

An army of scriveners has and is being employed, by obscure think-tanks mainly in Brussels, Washington and London. They are self-indulgently waving the 'neutral' flag, to show how 'consociational democracies' and 'partnership states' can tame nationalisms and ethnic wars, producing social harmony, peace and co-existence.[29] These scribes who, it should be said, began work in the late 1980s in earnest, saw their work mature in such texts as the Dayton accords (1995) and the Annan plan. But this trend is more general, and the theoretical and practical implications far broader and more serious.

The break-up of the Soviet Union had given rise to a set of US policies leading to the setting-up of garrison-prison states in East-Central Europe, Central Asia and the Middle East/Caucasus zones.[30] Not that this trend is a parthenogenesis pertaining to the end of the Cold War – far from that. In essence, it is a modern historical trend, which for the eastern Mediterranean region could be said to have been inaugurated in 1948 with the recognition of Israel. It then followed 1960–63 Cyprus – some could say in 1958 with the Macmillan plan[31] – and, in a more incisive and pervasive manner, in 1974 with the security formation of northern Cyprus in the wake of Turkey's invasions and the permanent stationing of its troops there. These types of state, whose formation is conducive to an organic and perpetual crisis caused by a complex articulation of external and internal agencies, are considered to be as much ethnically pure and militarily strong as possible. A garrison state highlights the position of 'the experts on violence' against that of the 'experts on business', to use Lasswell's terminology. In this respect, one could see the USA as a state with 'garrison-prison state' tendencies itself. In post-Cold War settings, this line of thinking is deemed to serve the USA and Israeli security interests in creating a range of buffer zones/enclaves regulated by friendly garrison states surrounding Russia and China, thus interposing between Russia and the French/German axis, on the one hand, and between Russia and China in Central Asia, on the other. We should also mention the most recent attempt to fragment the greater Middle East – two such cases being Afghanistan and Iraq – thus additionally serving Israeli interests. Iran and/or Pakistan may also follow suit. The post-Cold War predilection for garrison states only seems to be realised if the regime/state in question (e.g. Saddam's Iraq, Milosevic's Serbia) disobeys the suggestions of the global master, i.e. the USA. Turkey might also become a target of this US power calculus, given its large Kurdish population and its periodical opposition – at times really courageous – to US/Israeli ventures in Mesopotamia, Persia and the Levant. In our view, Cyprus falls within this analytical framework and historical trend: 'consociationalism', 'partnership states' and other such etiquettes are but intellectual exercises aiming at a sophisticated legitimisation of neo-imperial policy which, in a curious way, Israel/Palestine and Cyprus inaugurated for the Eastern Mediterranean during the Cold War.

The legal trajectory for a solution to the Cyprus issue since 1958–60 has been characterised by great power interference and imposition of illegal schemes alien to the interests of Cypriot society. In pedigree, the inserted constitutional triarchy in the arrangements of 1959–60, was merely a reflection of the British imperial policy of 'divide and rule' on the island during the EOKA struggle. The Treaties of Establishment, Alliance and Guarantee contravened the very charter of the UN. Article IV of the Treaty of Guarantee, signed on 16 August 1960, states that 'in the event of a breach of the present Treaty, Greece, Turkey and the UK undertake to consult together [...]. Insofar as common or concerted action may not prove possible, each of the three guaranteeing powers reserve the right to take action with the sole aim of re-establishing the state of affairs created by the present Treaty.' But this provision contravened article 2.4 of the UN Charter and was completely overridden by article 103. Article 2.4 states that 'all members [of the UN] shall refrain in their international relations from the threat or use of force against the territorial integrity or political independence of any state, or in any other manner inconsistent with the purpose of the UN'. Article 103 also affirms that 'in the event of a conflict between the obligations of the members of the UN under the present Charter and their obligations under any other international agreement, their obligations under the present Charter still prevail'.

Moving forward in time, the Ghali 'Set of Ideas' of 1992 was a step further to legitimising the partition work the British had begun in the 1950s. And the five Annan plans were the crowning of all such illegal efforts. Having reinforced the Treaties of Establishment, Alliance and Guarantee, Annan-V was over 9,000 pages long, complicated and muddled, and a true legal labyrinth poisoning the Cyprus *acquis* with all conceivable previous illegalities. The plan legitimised Britain's and NATO's colonial rights in and around Cyprus, while legally embedding Turkey's and Greece's security interests there. The Cypriots themselves were left separated into two garrison-prison statelets – what Annan, rather euphemistically, called 'constituent states of the United Cyprus Republic'. In this 45-year-old (il)legal trajectory and international imbroglio, only one UN plan made serious sense: that produced by UN mediator Galo Plaza in 1964–65. Turkey argued that it was pro-Greek Cypriot, but if it had been supported by Britain and the USA, it could have given a functional and fair solution to the island's problem of central governance, excluding both *enosis* and *taksim*. More to the point, the Plaza blueprint would not have contravened the charter of the UN, something which all schemes since 1959 have been doing, the Annan plan being the most outrageous and illegal of all. In other words: the Cypriot *acquis* over the decades has gone from bad to worse. It is little wonder that some have even tried to blend it with the European one, by way of legitimising substantive derogations.

As we saw earlier, the Hellenic plan was to achieve Cypriot EU membership, regardless of whether a solution to the island's division was found beforehand. Yet the Republic's entry to the EU could have been delayed until such time as Turkey received satisfaction on Cyprus, including its own EU membership. But Greece, breaking with its post-war subservient conservative traditions, threatened to veto the EU's eastward enlargement, so the thought was ruled out. This left one course open for the Anglo-Saxons: to use the UN to supervise talks between the Greek and the Turkish Cypriots, a process that kicked off at a G8 summit in summer 1999. It pointedly ignored both the legal Cypriot government and the UN Security Council itself. The Security Council simply came to rubber-stamp an Anglo-Saxon decision, committing Annan to initiate, oversee and conclude the process. Thus, in November of that year,

> Kofi Annan presented the two sides with a twenty-point 'non-paper' containing fundamental principles to guide the resolution of the problem. This 'non-paper' included the commitment that the comprehensive solution would be presented for ratification by separate and simultaneous

referenda in both communities. The referenda would provide through democratic means the legitimisation and approval of the comprehensive solution. The idea of the referenda was not new. It first appeared in 1992 in the secretary-general's 'set of ideas'. The referenda would be held on the outcome of the negotiated agreement on the Cyprus question. In 2004, however, the matter that was presented to the referendum vote was the disputed product of the secretary-general's arbitration and not the product of negotiations between the parties. [The shift] in the secretary-general's role from the offer of 'good offices' to arbitration was not apparent at the time.[32]

Strict timelines were set, the aim being to sort out Cyprus before it became a member of the EU.[33] The first plan was produced punctually by David Hannay and Tom Weston (the State Department's special coordinator on Cyprus), just a few weeks before the EU summit in Copenhagen (December 2002) – the venue where the EU would assess the outcome of negotiations with the Republic. A UN Peruvian functionary by the name of Alvaro De Soto fig-leafed the whole operation. The coordination among them was perfect – 'not a cigarette paper could have been slipped between their positions', Hannay said self-indulgently – but they miscalculated what a tough nut Cypriot society is to crack.[34]

Annan-I became Annan-II and then Annan-III in order to meet Turkish demands in a bout of horse-trading that was becoming increasingly inter-nationalised in the run-up to the war against Iraq. The Greek Cypriots, under Clerides until February 2003, accepted all three plans, but Denktash and Turkey did not. With its Middle Eastern role looming large, and with its generals restless not to concede more to the pro-European bloc led by Erdogan, Turkey's deep state realised that it was a good time for bargaining.

Turkey, under the new leadership of Tayyip Erdogan and Abdullah Gul, gave a new impetus to Turkish European diplomacy and vocation, presenting a mild, democratic and serene profile, as opposed to the macho politics of its previous, more or less, pro-Kemalist elites. This began winning over the Europeans, as the new ruling group in Turkey appeared willing to launch – and did – the kind of liberal reforms the Europeans wanted, particularly on human rights issues. Erdogan wanted a diplomatic solution to the Cyprus issue and appeared to be drifting away from the maximalist security positions of Denktash and the Turkish military. The Europeans liked it a lot, particularly the Left, but at the same time Turkey was under pressure from the USA to concede to American troops the right of passage, and flight from its south-eastern provinces to attack Saddam from the north. This Turkey opposed through a lack of votes in the Grand Assembly, but there was a general Turkish strategic calculus for this stance. The USA–UK, having enforced two no-fly zones in southern and northern Iraq in the 1990s, had at the same time assisted the Kurds in building their institutions in their northern regions, something that was anathema to the Turkish Kemalist elite. With the victorious Anglo-Saxon troops in northern Iraq in alliance with the Kurdish anti-Saddam forces of *peshmerga*, the Turks rightly changed their minds. The worst scenario for the Turkish Kemalist establishment would have been the initiation of a messy war, and a process whereby Iraqi Kurdistan could receive state recognition around a territory encompassing the oil-rich zones of Kirkuk and Mosul. It was a time of hard bargaining for Turkey, which at the same time wanted to streamline its financial crisis by seeking an IMF loan. Cyprus, once again, was used as a bargaining chip. State Department official Daniel Fried, in the presence of his colleague Mathew Bryza, spoke as follows to an audience of Greek Americans in Washington DC on 12 June 2003:

> When we were trying to persuade Turkey to allow the passage of our troops through its territory into northern Iraq, we offered Turkey two incentives: several billion dollars in grants and loans and Cyprus in the form of the Annan plan.[35]

Yet, despite the compromising stance of the Greek Cypriot side, none of the three plans satisfied the

Turkish overall strategic calculus. Indeed, Denktash, on instructions from Ankara, turned down all three versions, disappointing Clerides, the conservative President of the Greek-led Republic. Clerides accepted Annan-I as a basis for negotiation and indicated that he would be willing to accept Annan-II prior to the Copenhagen EU Council in December 2002. Annan-II came into being after Papadopoulos won the elections, against Clerides, in February 2003. It expired at the Hague the following month, again because of Denktash's intransigence. On 10 March 2003, Annan himself announced, 'we've come to the end of the road'. Well, not quite.

With the Greek-led Republic on the threshold of the EU, the Annan conception and its international cohort got on the move once again. They were assisted by the toppling of Denktash, giving hope to the Turkish Cypriots – and to Erdogan – that the Annan conception and its accompanying benefits could be endorsed. This, it should be noted, was strengthening Erdogan's democratic hand against Kemalism, certainly a highly desirable development for regional, European and global politics, but the Annan plan was supposed to solve the Cyprus issue, not the Turkish one.

But thus far, no serious negotiation had taken place between the Greek and the Turkish Cypriots; the UN arbitration was binding and all three plans were concocted; and this all was happening without any authorisation from the Security Council. As far as the EU was concerned, its influence in steering the Hannay–Weston–De Soto triumvirate was non-existent, despite the fact that all versions of the plan circumvented the European *acquis*, thus requiring insertion of unusual derogations – such as on freedom of settlement. Time was running out for Erdogan, who had made entry of Turkey into the EU the top priority of his cabinet. Yet, he had received two pledges from Romano Prodi, who had visited Ankara on 15 January 2004: 'a. Settling the Cyprus problem is not a precondition for Turkey's EU accession negotiations; b. whether a settlement is reached or not, the next step would be the lifting of the embargoes against the TRNC.'[36]

The Guarantor powers (Turkey, Britain, Greece) and their poor relatives, the Turkish and the Greek Cypriots, were summoned to the White House. Thus, a fourth edition of the plan was finalised by the Americans, while last-minute adjustments took place after the Bürgenstock meeting in Interlaken, Switzerland. There, Constantine Karamanlis junior, the nephew of Karamanlis who negotiated the 1959–60 settlements, applied some heavy pressure on Papadopoulos, the new President of the Republic of Cyprus and a Makarios loyalist in the latter's cabinets of the 1960s, to accept the plan. Thus, on the last day of March 2004, we

arrive at Annan-V, a non-negotiable item, which was
to be tested with the two separate referenda on 24
April, before the official entry of the Republic into the
EU on 1 May. But as far as procedure was concerned,
Annan-V was a case in point in itself. At Bürgenstock,
Turkey's Undersecretary at the Ministry of Foreign
Affairs, Ambassador Ugur Ziyal, handed over to De
Soto eleven points, without which Turkey and the
Turkish Cypriots would not sign the Annan-V. De
Soto succumbed to Turkish pressure and incorporated
all eleven points in the final version.[37] So much for
procedural matters. Substance was just as bad. What
did the Greek Cypriots turn down in the referenda of
24 April?

On the very day of the working class, 1 May, which
coincided with Cyprus's EU entry, the Republic would
have had to abolish itself and change its name, which
was tough for Papadopoulos and Christophias alike,
the latter being his powerful Communist ally, leading
the AKEL party, which once opposed the EC/EU as a
capitalist club. In its stead, two constituent states of
'equal status' would be formed – one Turkish and one
Greek Cypriot – subject to no hierarchy of laws and
administrative/executive units. The two states would
be called 'United Cyprus Republic' – as in a Spanish
wedding, the new appellation did not replace the old
but encompassed it.

The senate (the upper house) would be equally divided, 50:50, between Greek and Turkish Cypriots (this and many other points came straight from Ghali's 'Set of Ideas'). At the component level state, the lower house, seats would be 'distributed on the basis of the number of persons holding internal component state citizenship of each component state', provided that each such state 'shall be attributed a minimum of one quarter of the seats'.[38] That meant that the Turkish faction would be not less than 25 per cent of the total. Annan's scheme provided that parliamentary (lower house) decisions, in order to be valid, needed the approval of both houses, with a simple majority of members present and voting, including one quarter of senators present and voting from each constituent state. For particularly specified matters, a special majority of two-fifths of sitting senators, from each component state, would be required. Thus, as Kyriakides pinpoints, 'although the word veto does not appear in the Annan Plan, the Turkish Cypriot members of parliament will effectively have a veto over all legislative decisions if they voted *en bloc*'.[39] In this context, it is legitimate to argue that Turkey, via the political services of its Turkish Cypriot component state, could lay claims on the policy of Cyprus as a whole.

There would be no President or Prime Minister, but a 'Presidential Council' composed of four Greek

Cypriots and two Turkish Cypriots. They would have to be elected by a 'special majority', requiring two-fifths of each half of the senate. The rotating President of the Council would have no casting vote, carrying no special status as President of the Republic. All Council members 'shall be equal' and if they failed to reach consensus, then the Council would make decisions by simple majority, which in all cases must comprise at least one member from each component state. Time and again, and although the word 'veto' does not appear anywhere in the plan as in the 1959–60 constitutional arrangements, the Turkish members of the Council would effectively have had a veto if they voted *en bloc*. Disagreements and proceedings following vetoed items would be delegated to foreign arbitration: a Supreme Court, composed of three Turks, three Greeks and three foreigners would have to approve and decide upon a course of policy action.[40] There is no face-saving wash here – did anybody say that neo-colonialism cannot be so openly crude?

These deeply dysfunctional, cumbersome and destabilising provisions, encouraging all sorts of ethnic rancour and religious separatisms to flourish again and again, and aiding all kinds of wheeling and dealing between the regional powers in the ultimate service of neo-imperial hub-and-spoke arrangements, were topped up with the reinforcement of the illegal Treaties of Establishment, Alliance and Guarantee, which, among others: (a) concede the right to the Guarantor powers (Turkey, Britain and Greece) to intervene in the internal affairs of each constituent state; (b) concede the right to Britain to unimpeded access to the waters corresponding to the Sovereign Base Areas (SBAs) – these 'trampolines for Iraq' – as Perry Anderson called them – as well as in, around and over Cyprus; and (c) concede the right to Turkey to have permanently stationed troops on the island, with no guarantees for the enforcement of the provision for the withdrawal of the bulk of its troops over a period of years, in case Turkey had refused to do so for whatever conceivable reason – for instance if the Europeans blocked its EU membership.

Moreover, the menu of the Spanish wedding feast, included, importantly, the imposition upon the new 'consociational state' to drop all claims in the European Court of Human Rights; binding itself in advance to vote in favour of Turkey's entry into the EU; accepting a large number of Turkish settlers on Cyprus (creating a wonderful precedent for nearby Yisrael Beiteinu, the fifth largest party in Israel's Knesset and profoundly nationalistic); and impeding the exercising of fundamental property rights to the Greek Cypriot dispossessed and refugees, such as those of *jus utendi*, *jus fruendi* and *jus abutendi* in the

northern Cypriot areas under the jurisdiction of the
Turkish Cypriot component state, again in order to
maintain the character of a garrison-prison state. Last
but not least, the bill for the feast would have to be
paid by the wealthiest and the most prosperous Greek
Cypriots. The economic cost of the new 'partnership
state', conservatively estimated at between €30 billion
and €50 billion, which included compensation to
settlers wishing to return to Turkey, reconstruction of
cities such as Famagusta, would have eventually had
to be paid by the Greek Cypriot taxpayer. Here, one
could argue that the Greek Cypriot bourgeoisie was
doing a favour to the poor Turkish Cypriot, who was
suffering after so many years of trade embargo and
international isolation. But was he?

3

The 'Isolation' of Turkish Cypriots

HUMBUG CONTINUES

This is not a new theme at all in the *humbug* language of Anglo-Saxon diplomacy. Like the issue of the 'war on terror', present in all US and NATO documents since 1949, but elevated to the supreme status of the organising ideological principle of the Empire after 9/11, the 'lifting of the isolation of Turkish Cypriots' appeared first in the first half of the 1960s, only to be elevated as the 'international community's' chief concern after the Greek Cypriot rejection of what we described above as a 'plan'. For example, in a report by the UN Secretary-General dated 10 September 1964, we read:

Ever since the outbreak of violence on 21 December 1963, a variety of restrictions (...) have been imposed upon the

Turkish Cypriots. The isolation of Turkish Cypriots, due to the restrictions placed on their movements on the roads, brought hardship on the members of the community, as well as serious disruption of their economic activities (...). In addition to losses incurred in agriculture and in industry during the first part of the year, the Turkish Community had lost other sources of its income including the salaries of over 4,000 persons who were employed by the Cyprus Government and the public and the private concerns located in the Greek Cypriot zones. The trade of the Turkish Community had considerably declined during this period, due to the existing situation, and unemployment reached a very high level, as approximately 25,000 Turkish Cypriots had become refugees. Expenditure of the Turkish Communal Chamber on the development and other projects, as well as other expenditures, had dropped considerably (...).

And again in another report (8 December 1966), the Secretary-General stated:

Economically isolated, the Turkish Cypriot Community has found itself in a backwater as far as trade, industry and employment are concerned, and does not participate in the economic expansion of the country or the development of its resources. Many of the estimated 20,000 refugees and displaced persons in the Turkish Cypriot enclaves are unemployed, and their enforced idleness emphasises the isolation of the community, whose economy is sustained by financial assistance and relief supply from Turkey (...).

These reports, conveniently quoted by Rauf Denktash in his 1982 book, *The Cyprus Triangle*, constitute the premise upon which a *humbug* discourse on the subject has since developed, following the inter-communal strife of 1963–64, in the wake of Makarios's proposals for the amendment of the unworkable constitution.[41] But how could the UN, on the one hand, produce SC Resolution 186 and, on the other, recognise the need to put an end to the plight of the Turkish Cypriots by 'lifting their isolation'? Although this UN claim has taken on different meanings and nuances over the decades since it was first formulated, its contradictions have to be taken into consideration. The chief worry of Turkish nationalism on the island has since the late 1950s been the absorption of the poor Turkish Cypriot by the Greek capitalist, merchant, banker, tourist developer and landowner. Had this ever materialised, no hope for separate political institutions would have been possible for Turkish nationalism on the island. The 'international community' could endorse this concern while producing Resolution 186, not least because it endorsed the 1959–60 arrangements. As we affirmed earlier, *bullshitting, ambivalence* and *duplicity* go hand in glove.

Historically, two contrasting economic aims have developed on Cyprus, whose essence and scope are deeply political. Since 1956–57, the Turkish Cypriot political elite, with the full backing of the British, aimed at the separation of their own economy and ethnic/religious community from the Greek ones. By building separate economic institutions in tandem with political ones, their own garrison-prison state could emerge under the protection of Ankara, with the blessing of the Anglo-Saxon powers. The 'international community' placated the claim of Turkish nationalism in a variety of forms, one of which was the 'lifting of the isolation of Turkish Cypriots', an isolation which was entirely self-imposed. The Greek Cypriot side, being the ethnic majority on the island and in charge of all major capitalist activities in Cypriot society, has since 1960 been aiming at the integration/assimilation of the Turkish Cypriots within its own island-wide institutions, centrally run by the Government of Cyprus and by definition dominated by Greek Cypriots – although since 1974 the Greek side has been making further substantial concessions, particularly at the level of separate local government, the issue of settlers, recognition of political equality between the two communities etc. These are two *political projects* and not two social situations that spontaneously arose on Cyprus. Yet they should be analytically accepted only if two qualifications are attached to them:

1. The Greek Cypriot project for self-determination/ *enosis* was defined from within and mainly by the

Greek Cypriot bourgeoisie and the prosperous Church – with Cold War Makarios and post-Cold War Papadopoulos being its most prominent political exponents, although no Cypriot leader has since 1974 ever mentioned *enosis*. The Turkish Cypriot separation project was developed and defined from without, that is by Britain and then Turkey. In contrast to the Greek Cypriot case, which, as we saw earlier, was at crucial times severely undercut by mainland Greek policy, there has never been a Turkish Cypriot bourgeoisie, the result being that the Turkish Cypriot 'cause' is the product of external imposition. Hence the – rather justifiable – Greek Cypriot claim that the Turkish Cypriot political and negotiating elite has never been, nor is today, a free agent.[42]

2. Turkey's own project goes beyond the mere construction of a puppet Turkish Cypriot statelet on Cyprus. *Turkey's long-term security objective is the strategic control of the entire island, particularly its sea and air lanes, its seabed and large continental shelf, given that the Greek Cypriots constitute a mass ethnic body difficult to de-territorialise.* As defined by Menderes' special adviser on Cyprus in 1956, Nihat Erim, *taksim* is Turkey's minimum objective, the maximum being annexation and/or strategic control of the entire island by Turkey.[43] For this to

be achieved, Kemalist Turkey has been politically exploiting its minority on the island, as well as its international negotiating power. However, both the 1959–60 arrangements and the Annan plan (the right of veto, the right to military intervention etc.), despite the fact that they afforded Turkey enormous political advantages for the securitisation of the island according to its strategic interests, tended at the same time to contain Turkey's maximum objective by way of the British and mainland Greek (one could add the US and Israeli) presence in and around Cyprus. Yet, as we saw earlier, the Annan plan(s) included the possibility for Turkey to control the entire island via legal loopholes buried in the arrangements.

Some, including the UN, brush aside these kinds of facts and analysis, preferring instead to call all the above as 'two competing nationalisms on Cyprus' – so *humbug* continues. And now Britain and the USA are at pains to curtail Kemalism's maximum objective, the strategic control of the whole of Cyprus, via a condominium notion of power-sharing and Israel's powerful positioning in the region. For never mind how fundamentalist the Greek or the Turkish claims may sound, the fact remains that when scholarship has to pass judgement over two fundamentalisms, then, to avoid *humbug*, it should methodologically adhere to Isaac Deutscher's courageous statement made on the occasion of the 1967 Arab–Israeli war:

> On the face of it, the Arab-Israeli conflict is only a clash of two rival nationalisms, each moving within the vicious circle of its self-righteous and inflated ambitions. From the viewpoint of an abstract internationalism nothing would be easier than to dismiss both as equally worthless and reactionary. However, such a view would ignore the social and political realities of the situation. The nationalism of the people in semi-colonial or colonial countries fighting for their independence must not be put on the same moral-political level as the nationalism of the conquerors and oppressors.[44]

So scholarship supersedes *bullshit/humbug*, by distinguishing between the fundamentalism of the oppressed (the Greek Cypriot historical claim) and the fundamentalism of the oppressor (the neo-imperial claim propped up by Kemalism).

THE ARGUMENTS FOR AND AGAINST THE 'ISOLATION' THESIS

Just as there is so much repetition of 'lifting of the isolation of Turkish Cypriots' in the contemporary official parlance of the 'international community' after April 2004, so there is a large amount of *humbug* available.

From May 2004 onwards, Kofi Annan, in his Reports to the UN SC, repeatedly called for 'an end to the isolation of the Turkish Cypriots'.[45] Also the EU, through its General Affairs and External Relations Council and other bodies, has since 26 April 2004 been waving the same flag: 'To end the isolation of the Turkish Cypriots, establishing instruments of financial support for the economic development of the Turkish Cypriot community in the northern part of Cyprus in order to facilitate the re-unification of the island.'[46] Talat, the leftist leader of the Turkish Cypriots, is also tuned:

> What the Turkish Cypriots expect from the EU is quite clear: the EU keep its promises of direct aid for encouraging socio-economic investments and the start of direct trade with the ultimate goal of free trade in line with its own expressed will, as well as that of the UN Secretary-General's, in order to end the isolation of the Turkish Cypriot people.[47]

Intellectuals do not miss the feast, as they always – wrongly – hope for a free lunch. In a writing style that openly calls on Turkey to trade issues as if they were goods in a bazaar, Morton Abramowitz and Henri Barkey blame the EU for partly suspending entry talks with Turkey late in 2007 because of its refusal to open its ports to Greek Cypriot vessels. This is so wrong, they argue: 'Ankara is angry at the EU's failure to keep its promise to end the economic isolation of northern Cyprus and fears political upheaval at home if it lifts the ban with nothing gained.'[48]

The Greek Cypriots have been defensive and reactive, failing to grasp that the best defence against *humbug* is to opt out of its cultural zone. Instead of exposing and denouncing to the public the illegal Cypriot *acquis* accumulated over the decades in order to break away from it once and for all, they opted for producing power-point presentations about 'the myth of the isolation of Turkish Cypriots'.[49]

The Greek Cypriot counter-argument is that there is not so much isolation – which is true – and that the isolation that exists is the self-imposed result of 1963, of the Turkish invasions of 1974 and of the declaration of independence in 1983. The very tag 'isolation of Turkish Cypriots' is a misnomer, they argue, since there are more Turkish settlers in the North than Turkish Cypriots – which is also true. The demand-driven inefficient economic system and 'the large public sector of the occupied areas' has also been damaging to its economic performance. Furthermore, the Greek Cypriot argument goes, the dependence on Turkey and the influx of unskilled labourers from Turkey are detrimental to productivity.[50] Moreover, the Greek Cypriot side points to welfare policies implemented on the part of the Republic, including the issuing of tens of thousands of passports to Turkish Cypriots, the free welfare attention they receive and other benefits.[51] In short, the Greek Cypriots say that the Turkish Cypriots are using the 'isolation myth' in order to gain political capital, namely international recognition as a separate state – which might very well be true.

We argue, however, that this counter-discourse is, by and large, misleading. There is no Greek Cypriot talk about whether or not they will be accepting as a base for discussion, present or future, the illegal Cypriot *acquis* accumulated since 1958, beginning with Macmillan and ending with Annan. With a new left-wing President in charge, one would at least expect this question to be posed. It should be noted that this illegal Cypriot *acquis*, had it not been rejected in the referenda, would have become EU primary law.[52] Thus, the Greek Cypriot attitude since April 2004 has been one that is trying, reactively and defensively, to respond to *humbug* rather than to the big question of *what the next plan should be like*. We would assume that the Cypriot Left in particular, would want to step out of the Macmillan–Annan illegal orbit, as this leads Cypriot society nowhere, while deepening the dependence of European political and legal orders upon Anglo-Saxon power-political calculations. Some may argue that the 'Memorandum of Understanding' signed between the British premier, Gordon Brown, and the Communist President of the Greek-led Republic, Demetri Christofias, in June 2008 in London, marks a new beginning and goes beyond the British partitioning policies in Cyprus, adopting instead a unitary agenda. 'The UK will not support any move toward partition', says the Memorandum, and this is precisely *humbug* as *formal* partition would deprive Britain of its security rights in and around Cyprus.[53] Yet, and in order to make things even clearer, the Memorandum affirms Britain's role as a Guarantor power – Guarantor for itself, one should add, rather than for the Republic as a whole, as the 1974 events had shown – and affirms that any solution should be within the spirit of the signed 1960 Treaties. So has the official Cypriot Left opted to support a solution in Cyprus determined by the illegal Cypriot *acquis*? We do not know. Some Memos are public relations exercises and/or photo opportunities. Our duty here is to argue (and recommend) that the Cypriot Left, both in the North and the South of the island, should get out of this vicious circle of the illegal Cypriot *acquis*.

First, we will try to shed some light on the economic realities of northern Cyprus, by combining theoretical discussion and empirical findings. On this basis, we shall then make some suggestions as to how the developmental gap between the two separate parts of the island can be bridged, without falling into line with *humbug*. Finally, by way of a conclusion, we shall tackle the preconditions upon which Cyprus's post-imperial constitution should be drawn and based.

ECONOMIC TRENDS AND POLICIES

There is a considerable developmental cleavage between northern and southern Cyprus, north and south of the Attila line – euphemistically called the 'Green Line' by the UN. This hiatus differs in terms of history, form and political substance from other developmental gaps, such as that between centre and periphery in a given country (e.g. Greece, the UK), or between north and south, also in a given country (e.g. the gap between Italy's industrial north and agrarian/underdeveloped south).

From an economic perspective, Ugur's work – cited already – is one of the few serious academic studies of the North–South development gap in Cyprus.[54] Ugur suggested that under certain circumstances, EU membership for a unified Cyprus would be beneficial in driving economic growth and bringing about the convergence of per capita incomes in the northern and southern parts of the island. Having sketched out the body of analysis that points to increased economic well-being and, in particular, convergence of GDP per capita, Ugur, working on European Commission data, concluded that the empirical evidence supported the qualitative predictions of main economic theories. However, the magnitudes of the realised benefits in the statistical evidence reviewed by Ugur were small. Further, he anticipated that in order for these benefits to be fully realised, the institutional frameworks and governance structures, particularly in the northern areas where the *acquis* is suspended (henceforth: Areas of Suspended Acquis, ASA), needed to accommodate the liberalising reforms that are a condition of EU membership. Here, the nature of the economic arguments and how they come to be applied to Cyprus are briefly sketched out, and the circumstances examined.

The literature on integration predicts convergence of per capita GDP for the integrating countries or regions. However, the evidence also shows that income inequality within an integrating region may increase at the same time that region-wide income is converging with that of the other regions. The neoclassical growth model[55] and trade model[56] imply the convergence of the incomes of different regions over time. The neo-Marxist model of 'uneven development' does not apply at all in the case of Cyprus, simply because the developed Greek part of the island did not achieve growth at the expense of the Turkish one – as in the schemes of 'metropolis–periphery'.[57] In other words, neo-Marxist class analysis is rather irrelevant in examining the regional economic disparity in Cyprus.

In the growth model, regional incomes differ because of differences in capital–labour ratios and productivity. The EU's Single Market Programme, by making it easier for labour and capital to move across regional borders, facilitates a tendency towards the equalisation of capital–labour ratios, as both capital and labour seek to maximise their returns.[58] This means that poorer regions will initially grow at a faster rate than richer ones and, in this way, converge towards the income levels of the richer regions. But crucial in this respect, is the rate at which this convergence takes place as well as what drives it and what could finally impede it.

The trade model sees differences in factor endowments and prices as the underlying reason for differences in incomes. Regions specialise and trade on the basis of differences in factor endowments: as trade proceeds, the prediction is that factor prices across regions will tend to be equalised, with similar implications for income levels across regions. Yet evidence suggests that the authorities of ASA have imposed a high taxation regime on products imported from the Greek Cypriot sector, thus impeding mercantilism and supply-side integrative processes via island-wide trade activity.[59] At the same time, ASA authorities insist on direct trade with the EU, but following objections from the Republic of Cyprus, the EU has been discussing with the parties to allow direct trade only through the port of Famagusta, administered by Commission services and upon the authorisation of the Republic.

In the light of some of the actual experiences of divergence rather than convergence, the newer generation of growth models (the more recent adaptations of the neoclassical growth model) provide reasons as to why divergence rather than convergence may occur. These reasons centre on economies of scale of both an internal and external nature. In the former case, regions that are richer because of their larger physical and human capital holdings have this initial advantage compounded by increasing returns: in the main, they get the benefits of large-scale production.[60] In the latter case, divergences come about as the result of production centring itself – once integration begins – in particular regions in order to take advantage of servicing and other infrastructure.[61] This applies partly to the case of Cyprus, inasmuch as since 1963, and more substantially since 1974 the Turkish Cypriot economy has opted out of Greek-led economic institutions, whose huge advantage was their international integration and credibility.

The premise of Ugur's article was that Cyprus would join the EU at the very least as a federal entity. In the event, this was not the case, since in 2004 the island joined as the Republic of Cyprus – effectively, the Greek-led south,[62] and has more recently (January 2008) joined the euro zone. Given this premise, there was more cause to focus on the importance of institutions in view of the large public sector in ASA and the clientelistic relations predicated on it. In Ugur's (and the Greek Cypriots' view), the public sector's patronage in ASA would be inimical to the liberalising reforms (themselves an important factor in increasing economic prosperity in the longer term) that would be demanded by the EU. But this point of view has certain limits.

Some of the most clientelistic regimes in the world, such as those of Japan and the USA, are at the same time the most economically developed and technologically advanced. The same goes for the case of Italy, as well as some South-East Asian countries. Clientelism does not necessarily constitute an impediment to growth and modernisation. Bad management, however, whether Liberal or Keynesian, always does. We would argue that it is the type of management employed and the set of rules imposed on the manager and the managed by rationalised, regulatory and supervisory agencies which sets the tone. Clientelism and patronage may not be conducive to modernisation and growth, but they are not necessarily the source of every evil. In this context, the aid package of €139 million promised to ASA authorities may be absorbed in a manner pertaining to the reproduction of the existing (bad) management structures, which impede the initiation of processes of internationalisation, growth and island-wide cooperation.

It is in fact not entirely clear to what extent historically observed convergence elsewhere has been a consequence of joining the single market programme (SMP) or a consequence of redistribution through the funds provided by the EU. Here too, the story is mixed: while receipt of EU Structural Funds (SF) money can be positively correlated to gross value added (GVA) per capita in some countries, it is negatively correlated with GVA in others. Greece, for instance, experienced an economic slowdown in the 1980s, despite receiving large economic handouts from the EEC (Greece joined the Community in 1981). This is attributed to the pro-Keynesian management of Papandreou's cabinets, as against the trends defined by the processes of globalisation and European integration.[63] In Ireland, however, the experience was different: its entry into the EEC was followed by substantial modernisation and high per capita income generation. In Italy, among the first signatories of the Treaty of Rome in 1957, the economic gap between north and south of the country remains structurally unaltered.

In 1960, GDP per capita in today's ASA was 86 per cent of the Cypriot average, whereas in 1977, after the military invasions of the island, this ratio fell to 65 per cent and, by 1993, had dipped to 33 per cent. This widening gap was seen as the result of three factors: the inefficiency of institutions and government structures in northern Cyprus; the synchronisation (through the adoption of the Turkish lira) of ASA's economy with the Turkish business cycle; and the lack of recognition of the breakaway statelet. Being the result of a military operation resulting in the destruction of the Greek Cypriot-dominated business cycle, the economy of ASA had little choice but to fall back on large state interference in economic affairs and to integrate with Turkey, the politically dominant power.

Since 2001, inflation has fallen, but its downward trend has occasionally been disturbed by a depreciating Turkish lira. There were different responses to the trauma of 1974. The expansion of the public sector in ASA went hand in glove with its integration into the Turkish economy, whilst the Republic of Cyprus has encouraged entrepreneurship and export-led growth as well as developing structures that involve workers in social conflict resolution. ASA is participating in the internationalisation of its economy via its links with

Turkey, rather than with the Greek-led Republic, which Turkey has not recognised since 1963.

GDP growth in ASA in 2003 was 11.4 per cent; 15.4 per cent in 2004 and 10.6 per cent in 2005. This rate of growth, however, is most likely unsustainable: it is mostly demand-driven and based on tourism and construction (this sector averaged annual growth of circa 21 per cent over the period), lacking a sound structural basis. In its 'Guide to Foreign Investors', by ASA's State Planning Organisation, we read:

> The fixed capital investments have been 645,460,056 YTL at current prices in 2005. The public sector financed 27% of total fixed investments and the remaining 73% was financed by the private sector. Public services and transportation sectors constituted the biggest shares of the public sector investments. The shares of public sector investments have been 53% and 26,8% respectively. On the other hand, private sector investments have been intense with 43,1% in dwelling and with 11,7% in manufacturing sectors [...] Under the Incentive Law, 290 incentive certificates have been granted until the end of 2006 [...] Tourism sector has the highest share in fixed investments and this sector occupies 69,7%.[64]

The informal sector of the economy is thought to be also very large and impossible to estimate with any confidence, whereas finances collapsed in 2000–01, after a liquidity crisis in Turkey and the collapse of the lira. Per capita income grew to 76 per cent of ASA GDP in 2004[65] and, currently, the average Greek Cypriot is twice as wealthy as the Turkish Cypriot, with gross national product per capita of $23,000 and $12,367 respectively.[66] ASA's economy has also benefited, although not massively, from the lifting of restrictions across the 1974 cease-fire line imposed by Turkey, as well as the EU's 'Green Line' regulation, introduced in April 2004.[67] This latter was put forward by the EU in order to address the issue of the suspension of the *acquis* in northern Cyprus and contribute to the 'lifting of the isolation of Turkish Cypriots'. Figure 1 shows the growth rates of GDP for the two halves of

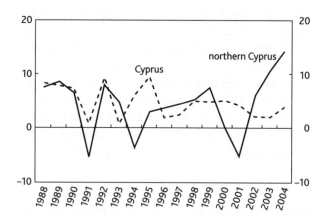

Figure 1　Real GDP growth in Cyprus and northern Cyprus, 1988–2004

Source: The Republic of Cyprus, Ministry of Finance 2006.

the island: northern Cyprus clearly exhibits greater volatility in its rate of growth.

This is despite the fact that ASA is continuing to receive considerable financial aid from the Turkish mainland: in 2005, Turkey signed an agreement to provide ASA with financial assistance, to the tune of US$450 million. In 2006 circa 15 per cent of ASA GDP was received from Turkey. This amount of money is considerably higher than that pledged by the EU, yet Turkey seems unable to contribute to catching up with the Greek-led Cyprus. Given the badly managed institutions of ASA, its public finances would be in a parlous state without such assistance. Between 2000 and 2003, ASA's average budget deficit was around 17 per cent of GDP, while the average inflation rate for the same period was 42 per cent.[68] Though ASA has a larger agricultural sector, the differences in composition of GDP by sector (between ASA and the Republic) are not marked: the services sector accounts for the lion's share of GDP in both cases, although Greek Cypriot services are qualitatively more advanced and modern. Cyprus has traditionally educated a large proportion of its population through high school graduation and beyond – human capital is often stressed as an important factor in the newer generation of growth models.[69] Time and again, however, this applies mainly to Greek Cypriots, partly to Turkish Cypriots and only rarely to the illegal Turkish settlers. The significant immigration of unskilled settlers from Turkey in parallel with the outflow of skilled labour (mainly to Western Europe and Britain, in particular) has altered the labour profile in a way that has been detrimental to labour productivity in ASA. The divergent paths of labour productivity in ASA and the Greek-led Republic of Cyprus can clearly be seen in Figure 2.

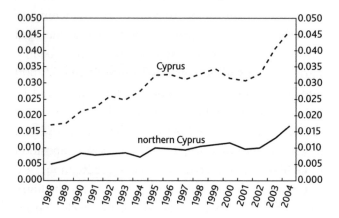

Figure 2 Labour productivity in Cyprus and northern Cyprus, 1988–2004

Source: The Republic of Cyprus, Ministry of Finance 2006.

Cyprus lacks natural resources, and the importance of tourism means that GDP can vary significantly with changes in tourism income. Cyprus is therefore the classic small island economy of economics literature. If one views the often-cited 'economic isolation' of ASA within the context of economic growth theory, then a significant factor might be thought to be the difficulty ASA has in attracting investment. In a statistical examination of the factors driving growth in ASA between 1977 and 1996, Ghatak and Fethi (1999)[70] found that physical and human capital have had long-term effects on economic growth in ASA. Although their findings have to be qualified because of the small set of observations used, they do provide some support for physical and human capital as important drivers of growth. It is undoubtedly the case that various instruments of financial intercourse in ASA are blunted by its non-recognition. For a small island economy, to quote Ghatak and Fethi (1999), 'the constraints become even stricter when there is inefficiency in employing these limited resources, which in turn affects the [sic] output and economic growth'.[71] Size matters: the population of ASA was 145,000 in 1977 – thousands of settlers had in the meantime poured in – 212,000 by 2001 and nearly 270,000 today (early 2008 estimates by ASA's State Planning Organisation). Given the exodus of Turkish Cypriot workers to London and other parts of Europe, the incoming labour force to ASA hardly contributes to productivity and growth, as it is unskilled, uneducated and idle. It should also be said that the issue of non-recognition puts off a range of investors because of uncertainty, but not all investors. UK banks, such as Barclays, have opened branches in ASA, and the port of Famagusta exports Turkish Cypriot commodities all over the world, and also operates a regular ferry service with Syria.[72] Moreover, ASA authorities keep expanding their economic services around the Middle East, a recent prominent case being the opening of a trade office in Israel.[73] Turkish Cypriot society, despite its antipathy towards the Anatolian settler – there is clearly a cultural clash – is also culturally alert, modernistic and tuned to European and Greek Cypriot mores and social attitudes. Their inclination to learn and communicate with others not only in English and Turkish, but also in Greek, serves them well, and is something which the average Greek Cypriot, wrongly, does not aspire to. It is a fact that Turkish Cypriot society, including those settlers who have integrated over the years, is happy to embrace its Greek Cypriot counterpart, learning from the mistakes of the past.

From a purely economic perspective, however, three things emerge:

1. There is a development gap between ASA and the Greek-led Republic of Cyprus, which does not

necessarily amount to an 'isolation of Turkish Cypriots', but to a partial *economic underdevelopment* between *ASA as a region* and the rest of the Republic. Income differentials between the average Greek and Turkish Cypriot are diminishing, and if the huge black sector economy operating in ASA is taken into account, then the discrepancy between the average income of the Turkish Cypriot (excluding the settlers) and the Greek Cypriot may not be at all pronounced. ASA, as a region, is internationalised via Turkey, enjoying a variety of economic benefits and aid. As a territory, it is small in size and population, and it is doubtful that ASA's political recognition would accrue the expected economic benefits. In this respect, from a purely economic point of view, the best prospect for ASA is economic integration with the Republic of Cyprus within the EU.

2. In ASA, the institutional and management culture militates against the type of change and capitalist modernisation that a small (open) island economy needs to undergo to reach its potential. From an economic perspective, the performance of ASA matters because stifled capital accumulation for ASA drags down the economy of the island as a whole. When this latter factor is considered in the context of Turkey's patronage and the impediments

to island-wide trade imposed by Turkey for the purpose of keeping the two economies separated, then the hope is to keep pushing for facilitating agreements on trade between the two parts of the island as well as assisting the EU *and* the Republic of Cyprus to develop comprehensive investment and trade policies towards ASA.

3. In this context, the problems of institutional and governance structures mismanaged by Turkey and referred to by Ugur, including our comparative qualifications, seem to have some resonance. Furthermore, it is certainly true that by freeing itself from the vagaries of the Turkish lira and officially tying itself to the euro *and* the Republic of Cyprus, the economy of ASA can quickly buy itself an international economic credibility that will help facilitate foreign direct investment. Defying their political elite, Turkish Cypriot society is already embracing the euro and the Republic's benefits.

Conclusion

We have aimed at providing a non-partisan approach to the Cyprus issue today, that goes beyond the conservative perceptions of certain ruling elites on the island and their NATO masters, that is, above all the UK, the United States, Turkey and Greece. We have dealt with a number of historical and political themes pertaining to Cyprus, its constitution and imperial politics. It should be to nobody's surprise that, as shown in our narrative, themes such as 'the isolation of Turkish Cypriots', the Annan plan or the entry of Turkey into the EU, are strictly interlinked.

We have seen, however, that a fundamental prerequisite for achieving such a state of post-imperial affairs on Cyprus is the defeat of the dominant discourse about Cyprus. Over the years, a *humbug* discourse has conscientiously been developed around the Cyprus issue and the Cypriot constitution by all sorts of intellectuals, journalists and activists seeking to justify the actions of their imperial political classes. *Humbug* is not a lie. It is something far more serious and dangerous. It is the conscientious attempt of the dominant ideology to produce such forms of mass subjecthood, which will reflect the scope of the *humbug*: indifference to, and/or distortion of the truth and subservience to imperial rule as the only rule.

Bullshitting about Cyprus is abundant, beginning with the so-called two quasi-nationalisms on the island, presumably the 'innate' product of the historical hatred between the Turk and the Greek, as if the Greek nationalism of the eighteenth and nineteenth centuries was a parthenogenesis of the southern Balkans, or as if the Greek campaign in Asia Minor was the product of an independent drive of the 'imperial' Greek state to conquer Anatolia. Nothing of the sort. Greek nationalism, as all other Balkan nationalisms, was the product of the European Enlightenment and became a political force in order to serve primarily the interests of Britain and France in the eastern Mediterranean, as against those of the Russians.[74] Similarly, Venizelos's push into Asia Minor was but a British proxy war to partition Turkish Anatolia according to the secret schemes agreed in 1916–17. Turkey and Greece stood between the Empires of the West (Britain, France) and the East (Russia). The Anglo-French work was to periodically pit the Greeks against the Turks, as well as other Balkan states, when it suited them, according to historical circumstances and the imperial interests at stake.[75]

The first mistake of scholars examining the origins of Turkish Cypriot nationalism is that they interpret sporadic pro-Kemalist statements made by a minority Muslim elite in the 1930s as a mass, political, national identity sign. But nationalism is meaningful only if it refers to mass political mobilisation, and this happened in Cyprus only at British instigation in the 1950s. Had Britain not pitted the Turks against the Greeks, both at societal (the formation of Turkish Cypriot auxiliary police) and political (the tripartite Conference) levels, the evolution of the Muslim identity in Cyprus at a mass level would have been different. More to the point, had Britain not encouraged Turkey to enter Cyprus, then Turkish policy in Cyprus might have followed paths totally different from those pursued. We should also mention here that the Muslims of Cyprus had no sympathy with Kemal's secularism, so one can imagine what an extra effort it took for Britain and Turkey to politicise Cypriot Muslims on the basis of a nationalistic programme.

The *humbug* discourse on this subject – as exemplified in the Report of the International Crisis Group on Cyprus, which we quoted in Chapter 1 – does not care very much for the aforementioned discussion. Humbuggers are not interested in approaching the truth. They are only interested in *bullshitting*, that is, creating images that are reified in the minds and actions of individuals in a way that serves the interests of the dominant, imperial powers. Behind *bullshit*, there is usually a political agenda. In this case, the agenda is that these two peoples, the Greek and the Turkish Cypriots, cannot live together, and can live in peace only if separated and piled up into two different statelets on an island of 9,251 sq. km, 277 sq. km of which constitutes the sovereign colonial territory of the British military bases. *Humbug* talk makes this outdated imperialism and political anachronism sound like something normal.

Most, if not all, of the *humbug* discourse about Cyprus, past and present, is due to the imperial acts of omission and commission accumulated in the constitution of Cyprus since the late 1950s – what we called here the *Cypriot acquis*. The Cypriot *acquis* is the result of Anglo-Saxon cherry-picking from the body of legal texts, treaties, UN SC Resolutions, and UN General Assembly Resolutions, which Annan's patch-up work tried to incorporate into a document more than 9,000 pages long. This document, upon which the Cypriot society was supposed to pass judgement, became available on the UN's website only a few hours before the referenda. We emphasise that this selection is partial, because it is defined by the class and national interests of Anglo-Saxon powers, the dominant powers in the eastern Mediterranean, without taking into account Cypriot society. For instance, Galo Plaza's ideas in his 1965 Report figure nowhere in the plan, nor do the UN's General Assembly resolutions. *The Annan plan was an Anglo-Saxon imperial plan, not the product of a French–German design of peaceful economic expansion.*

A *humbug* discourse was employed in support of the plan, precisely because it served the geo-strategic calculus of Britain and the USA to re-fashion the greater Middle East on the basis of garrison-prison states. France, Russia, China and Germany had to go along with it, despite their private reservations. And it was *humbug* because it tried to present as something 'normal', 'sensible' and in a condensed form, the illegalities of over 45 years of imperial machinations camouflaged as 'United Nations plan'. Cyprus was not, and is not, Iraq. Iraq was a different ball-game altogether: the stakes in Mesopotamia and the Gulf region were and are much higher for all concerned, so all Eurasian powers surmised that opposition to war had to be aired inside and outside the UN. Turkey behaved very bravely under Erdogan by not allowing US and British troops to cross its territory to attack Saddam from the north, but it, too, has to make a choice. It could either enter the re-partition game of Middle Eastern and

Central Asian states and regions putting in jeopardy its own territorial integrity in the future, or denounce these imperial undertakings and embrace its Eurasian allies, from France eastwards to Russia and China. Cyprus, Thrace and the Aegean are some of Turkey's testing grounds (others are Syria, Armenia and Iraqi/Persian Kurdistan): de-securitising its policy towards Greece and Cyprus, Turkey could assist in the democratisation of its immediate periphery while entering the EU (Greece supports Turkey's EU bid).

But the EU as a whole – including Britain, Denmark, the Visegrad countries et al., and not just France – should re-think its stance on the Cyprus question and stop slavishly following the USA. If the Annan plan had been approved by Cypriot society, then it would have become primary law of the EU. Given its unique and unparalleled set of derogations and co-federal provisions (restriction on the three freedoms, the issues of settlers and property, the continuation and reinforcements of the Treaty of Guarantee and so on), then possible candidates for future entry into the EU, such as the Ukraine, would have ended up discussing partition/co-federation between the East (pro-Russian) and the West (pro-USA) of the country, rather than the entry of a sovereign state whose weight would strengthen the power of the EU. Entry of co-federal states into the EU is a deeply destabilising factor for its political cohesion as it expands eastwards and tries to incorporate its neighbours into its structures (viz. the EU's 'neighbourhood policy'). But this prospect, obviously, favours the Anglo-Saxon project, which aims at expanding the EU as much as possible on neo-conservative/neo-liberal economic grounds, thus further loosening its central political structures and cohesion. In other words, acceptance of the Annan plan would have meant further undermining of the Franco-German project for the political unification of Europe. From this perspective, both the EU and the Republic of Cyprus should demand a re-start of negotiations on the basis of the European *acquis communautaire*. Turkey, for the reasons stated above, should also embrace this perspective. Indeed, there is common ground for all interested parties to converge for 'a just and lasting solution to the Cyprus question'.

Unfortunately, however, soon after the referenda of 24 April 2004, the EU espoused *humbug* talk: 'to lift the isolation of Turkish Cypriots to help the re-unification of the country'. It is not difficult to understand why the UN resorts to *humbug*, but why does the EU? With respect to this theme, we have shown here a couple of things: first, the developmental gap between ASA and the Republic has been reduced and can be further reduced, without the need to employ *humbug*; second, that the Republic and the EU should try simultaneously to cooperate, in every possible economic manner, to bridge the regional economic disparity between ASA's and the Republic's territories, while advancing island-wide economic and political integration. Direct trade between ASA authorities and the EU can and must happen, as long as the Republic is involved in that process within the framework of a more general effort to integrate the economy of the entire island and end its vivisection. This will serve both Cypriot communities and the EU project for political unification of the continent.

A major theme of this book has been to reveal what imperial powers and their intellectuals know *in private*, but hide *in public*, through their refined and sophisticated *humbug* talk. But we have used a cliché, which is widespread particularly among Greek Cypriot politicians: we have talked of 'a just and lasting solution to the Cyprus problem', immediately opening up the possibility that we too are talking *humbug*. For it would be bourgeois *humbug* if the Cypriot Left, now in office, fails to meet the condition hereunder, on the basis of which our conception of a *Cypriot post-imperial constitution* is structured. And as far as Cyprus after imperialism is concerned, this much is clear to us for the future: Cyprus, guided by its society and its parties of the Left, should begin moving now, nationally and internationally, outside the perimeters of its illegal and externally imposed imperial *acquis*. In other words, the Cypriot Left should convince itself that – with apologies to Marx – the liberation of Cyprus will only be the work of Cypriots themselves.

Notes

1. On this form of creation of subjecthood, see Terry Eagleton, *The Ideology of the Aesthetic*, Oxford 1990, p. 24, passim.
2. Harry G. Frankfurt, *On Bullshit*, Princeton 2005, pp. 14 ff., passim. Frankfurt is Professor Emeritus of analytical philosophy at Princeton University.
3. ICG Report No. 190, 'Cyprus: Reversing the drift to partition', Brussels, 10 January 2008, p. 1.
4. Michael Emerson and Nathalie Tocci, *Cyprus as a Lighthouse of the East Mediterranean: Shaping Re-unification and EU Accession Together*, CEPS, Brussels 2002, pp. 7, 31. The concept of 'cosociationalism' is discussed below.
5. Fred Halliday, 'Cyprus risky stalemate', 29 August 2007, www.opendemocracy.com
6. Rauf R. Denktash, *The Cyprus Triangle*, London 1982, p. 13.
7. The legal and political orchestra of the 'international community', including such UK diplomats as David Hannay, and such Swiss legal advisers as Didier Pfirter, drafted five plans in order to meet Turkish and British demands vis-à-vis Greek-led Cyprus's impeding accession to the EU and the Anglo-Saxon attack on Iraq. We shall examine below the linkages between the 2002–04 international juncture and the contours of the Annan Plan, a legal labyrinth of over 9,000 pages of text over which the Greek and the Turkish Cypriots were to pass separate judgements, just a few hours after these 9,000 pages became fully available online (on the website of the UN). Some 65 per cent of Turkish Cypriots voted in favour, whereas 76 per cent of Greek Cypriots rejected it.

8. Article 16 of the Treaty of Lausanne reads as follows: 'Turkey hereby renounces all rights and titles whatsoever over or respecting the territories situated outside the frontiers laid down in the present Treaty and the islands other than those over which her sovereignty is recognised by the said Treaty, the future of those territories and islands being settled by the parties concerned.'

9. The best works on the British policy of 'divide and rule' in Cyprus are by Robert Holland and William Mallinson, two accomplished historians whose scholarly work has shed light on many substantive issues of British policy in Cyprus in the 1950s and beyond: Holland, *Britain and the Revolt in Cyprus*, Oxford 1998; and Mallinson, *Cyprus: A Modern History*, London 2005.

10. On this topic, see the PhD dissertation by Paschalis Kitromilides, an anti-nationalist researcher of Cypriot origin and now Professor of the history of political ideas at the University of Athens, *Tradition, Enlightenment and Revolution*, PhD dissertation, Harvard University, 1978, as well as his '"Imagined communities" and the origins of the national question in the Balkans', in M. Blinkhorn et al. (eds), *Modern Greece: Nationalism and Nationality*, London 1990, p. 34, passim. Niyazi Kizilyrek, Bülent Evre and others bring some evidence of Turkish Cypriot nationalist trends before the 1950s. These trends, nevertheless, are marginal and without the intellectual critical mass or the material means to affect large Turkish Cypriot strata, thus effecting independent nationalist policies in favour of Turkey. It should be noted that Muslims/Turkish Cypriots were largely uneducated and poor and, as Kizilyrek does not fail to mention, their contribution to Cyprus's national wealth was rather unimportant; see his *Cyprus: The Deadlock of Nationalisms* (in Greek), Athens 1999, pp. 84–5, passim; Bülent Evre, *Kibris Türk Milliyetçiliği: Oluşumu ve Gelişimi*, Nicosia 2004, pp. 90–105, passim. *Students of Turkish Cypriot nationalism confuse the isolated and piecemeal pro-Kemalist*

statements of Turkish Cypriot elites from 1931 onwards with
the political project of the British to radicalise Turkish Cypriots
en masse, thus transforming an elite Kemalism on Cyprus into
a mass nationalistic project of political mobilisation via Turkish
policy. Without British instigation and active participation in
the forming of a Turkish policy in Cyprus, Turkey would never
have entered the Cyprus question the way it did – if it had
entered it at all.

11. Perry Anderson, 'The divisions of Cyprus', *London Review of
     Books*, 24 April 2008.

12. The usual excuse for Greece's pathetic policy is the plight of the
     country after the German occupation and the bloody civil war.
     This excuse does not stand up. Greece accepted her status as
     a protectorate of the USA in 1947, at a time when the British
     Empire was going from crisis to crisis, not to mention the
     conflict between Britain and the USA over the Suez Canal affair.
     The Greek political elite was not in a position to capitalise on
     any of these inter-allied conflicts, making political capital for
     Cyprus, simply because of the subservient and conservative
     will of its rulers.

13. See, Van Coufoudakis, *Cyprus: A Contemporary Problem in
     Historical Perspective*, Minnesota 2006, pp. 73 ff.

14. We should not fail to mention here the significant contribution
     by Diana Weston Markides, *Cyprus 1957–63: From Colonial
     Conflict to Constitutional Crisis; The Key Role of the Municipal
     Issue*, Minnesota 2001.

15. An excellent work on this topic is by Claude Nicolet, *United
     States Policy towards Cyprus, 1954–1974*, Mannheim 2001. See
     also, Ian Craig and Brendan O'Malley, *The Cyprus Conspiracy*,
     London 1999. It is important to note that Martin Packard, a
     British naval intelligence officer serving in Cyprus and working
     towards bringing the two communities together, recalls being
     asked to take visiting US politician, acting Secretary of State,
     George Ball, around the island in 1964. Arriving back in
     Nicosia, says Packard, 'Ball patted me on the back, as though

I were sadly deluded and he said: That was a fantastic show son, but you've got it all wrong, *hasn't anyone told you that our plan here is for partition?*' (our emphasis). See, http://news. bbc.co.uk/2/hi/europe/4632080. We are thankful to a Greek Cypriot diplomat who drew our attention to this source (he wishes to remain unidentified). Packard develops in full his personal witness in his *Getting it Wrong: Fragments from a Cyprus Diary 1964*, Milton Keynes 2008.

16. *New Left Review*, November–December 2003. It should be noted that during the war, the term United Nations was used to denote those states which were allied against the axis powers. On the crucial international juncture 1943–45, see the seminal work by Gabriel Kolko, *The Politics of War*, New York 1968.

17. Kennan's containment theory argued for a strong Germany and Japan, both of which would be harassing a domestically weak USSR from each end of Eurasia, thus eventually making it collapse. Instead, Acheson and his right hand man, Paul Nitze, who took over from Kennan the Policy Planning office of the State Department and supervised the authorship of the famous NSC-68 document, argued for a 'hub and spoke' system of global governance, whereby Washington constituted the hub and all other states/capitals, particularly of developed capitalism, made up the dependent spokes. The instruments to achieve this neo-imperial undertaking in Western Europe and SE Asia, were NATO and, as far as SE Asia was concerned, bilateral treaties (e.g. the treaty with Japan). Moreover, Acheson and Nitze argued, by creating structures of dependency within the polities of the allies, an insurance policy for Washington was automatically generated, as these allies would never be in a position to challenge the global supremacy of the US, as well as its security interests around the globe (e.g. its position in the Middle East). We have argued elsewhere that the neo-imperial model of the USA, coupled with the centrality of the dollar in global currency markets and trade, is deeply Achesonian in

nature and has since the 1940s been the central pillar of the US neo-imperial system of governance; see Vassilis K. Fouskas and Bülent Gökay, *The New American Imperialism*, Connecticut 2005.

18. Turkish political nationalism in Cyprus, as best exemplified by Denktash and others, argues that Turkey received assurances by the USA and Britain that, by 'Government of Cyprus', is meant the bi-communal state established in 1960. Denktash himself regrets this resolution because he knows that this interpretation does not stand up – see Michael Moran (ed.), *Rauf Denktash at the United Nations: Speeches on Cyprus*, Cambridge 1997, pp. 13–14.

19. The basic account on this is by Justice Dekleris, *The Cyprus Issue 1972–1974: The Last Chance* [in Greek], Athens 1981. Turkish Professor Aldikacti also confirms this – see Van Coufoudakis, *Cyprus*, p. 120, note 18.

20. Glafkos Clerides, *My Deposition*, v.3, Nicosia 1997, pp. 342–3.

21. Christopher Hitchens, *The Trial of Henry Kissinger*, London 2001.

22. On this issue, see the perceptive essay by Marios L. Evriviades, 'The US and Cyprus: The politics of manipulation in the 1985 UN Cyprus High level meeting', Occasional Research Paper no. 3, Institute of International Relations, Athens 1992.

23. See Fouskas's work: 'Uncomfortable questions: Cyprus, October 1973–August 1974', *Contemporary European History*, 2005; 'US foreign policy in the Greater Middle East during the Cold War and the position of Cyprus', in Vassilis K. Fouskas and Heinz A. Richter (eds), *Cyprus and Europe: The Long Way Back*, Mannheim 2003; 'The imprint of Dumbarton Oaks on Cyprus', *Hellenic Studies*, 2004.

24. It is useful to remember here that Britain's Foreign Secretary, Robin Cook, publicly urged the Turkish Cypriots to accept the invitation – see, http://www.un.int/cyprus/pr170398.htm

25. Alan Makovsky, 'Turkey's faded European dream', paper presented to the Conference 'The Parameters of partnership: Germany, the US and Turkey', American Institute for Contemporary German Studies, The Johns Hopkins University, Washington DC, 24 October 1997, p. 52. See also, Gülnur Aybet, 'Turkey's long and winding road to the EU: Implications for the Balkans', *Journal of Southern Europe and the Balkans*, April 2006, pp. 65–83.

26. Zaim M. Necatigil, *The Cyprus Question and the Turkish Position in International Law*, Oxford 1996, pp. 234–8. This is a source that should be quoted, because it incidentally draws the reader's attention to the progressive advancement of the Turkish negotiating position over the years at the expense of the Greek one.

27. Van Coufoudakis, 'Cyprus, the United States and the United Nations since 1960', *Hellenic Studies*, Autumn 1994, p. 47. The 'three freedoms' are those of movement, settlement and ownership.

28. The full text is available online. See also, Andreas P. Kyriacou, *A Viable Solution to the Cyprus Problem: Lessons from Political Economy*, Nicosia 2003, pp. 92–209.

29. Arend Lijphart, among others in the 1970s and 1980s, unaware of how his writings would be exploited, kicked off the discussion on 'consociationalism' – see his *Democracies: Patterns of Majoritarian and Consensus Government in Twenty-one Countries*, New Haven 1984.

30. On the concept of the 'garrison state', see Harold Lasswell, *Essays on the Garrison State*, edited and with an introduction by Jay Stanley, New Brunswick 1997. The concept was put forward by Lasswell in the late 1930s in an essay entitled 'Sino-Japanese crisis: The garrison state versus the civilian state', and was further elaborated in his 'The garrison state' essay, published in the *American Journal of Sociology* in January 1941. Lasswell develops the thesis that 'perpetual crisis is likely to reverse the trend of historical development *from* progress

toward a world commonwealth of free men, *toward* a world order in which the garrison-prison state reintroduces caste bound social systems'.

31. We would like to point out that the Macmillan Plan was quickly rejected by Makarios, describing the idea of 'partnership' as imposition of a 'triple condominium' on Cyprus. It is also significant to remember that the Labour opposition at the time criticised the plan as deeply divisive.

32. Van Coufoudakis, *Cyprus*, pp. 28–9. Coufoudakis, one of the most solid exponents of the 'anti-Annan camp', despite giving powerful arguments in favour of rejection, fails to put forth a comprehensive alternative *outwith* the historical illegal perimeter crystallised in the plan.

33. We follow here the narrative by Claire Palley, *An International Relations Debacle: The UN Secretary-General's Mission of Good Offices in Cyprus, 1999–2004*, Oxford 2005, pp. 23 ff. This account, deeply pro-Greek, is nevertheless accurate in its blow-by-blow description of events and remains the only one available for consultation in English to date.

34. Hannay's version of events is deeply flawed and one-sided – truly a *humbug* must-read, see his *Cyprus: The Search for a Solution*, London 2005.

35. *Cyprus Weekly*, 5–11 August 2005, p. 52. I am grateful to Marios Evriviades for drawing my attention to this source – see also his review of Claire Palley's work in *Mediterranean Quarterly*, spring 2006, pp. 87–91.

36. Quoted in Palley, *An International Relations Debacle*, pp. 97–100.

37. Claire Palley's work makes reference to all of these points, the most important of which, in our view, was the maintenance of Greek and Turkish troops on the island even after the accession of Turkey into the EU; see, Palley, ibid., p. 259.

38. Klearchos A. Kyriakides, 'Legitimising the illegitimate? The origins and objectives of the Annan Plan', in Van Coufoudakis and Klearchos A. Kyriakides, *The Case Against the Annan Plan*, London 2004, p. 25. Kyriakides's criticism of the illegalities of the Annan schemes is one of the most accurate accounts available to date – the author is a practising solicitor and a Senior Lecturer in Law at the University of Hertfordshire.

39. Ibid.

40. Other key institutions in which foreign nationals would have had important powers included the Reconciliation Commission, the Central Bank, the Relocation Board, the Property Court and the organs of the Property Board.

41. Denktash, *The Cyprus Triangle*, pp. 37–8, 46–7.

42. Turkish Cypriot liberal intellectuals and sections of the Left are in total agreement on this with the Greek side; see in particular Jon Hemming (Reuters), 'North Cyprus: Tied to "motherland"', *Kathimerini* (English edition – insert in *International Herald Tribune*), 9 August 2000, p. 2.

43. We have ample historical evidence for this Turkish policy – see, for example the works by Makarios Drousiotis (*The Dark Side of EOKA*, in Greek, Athens 1999), Ioannis Stefanides (*Isle of Discord*, London 1999), Neoklis Sarris (*The Other Side*, in Greek, Athens, multiple editions) and many others.

44. Isaac Deutscher interviewed by Alexander Cockburn, Tom Wegraf and Peter Wollen, 'On the Israeli-Arab war', *New Left Review*, 1967.

45. See, for instance, Report of the Secretary-General on the United Nations Operations in Cyprus, S/2004/437, S/2006/931 and S/2007/699.

46. Among others, European Council-General Affairs Council, 'EU financial support for the Turkish Cypriot community', Brussels, 6810/06 (Presse 60), 27 February 2006.

47. Mehmet Ali Talat, 'Turkish Cypriots' expectations from the European Union', *Turkish Policy Quarterly*, Fall 2005, available at http://www.devplan.org/Frame-eng.html

48. Morton Abramowitz and Henri Barkey, 'Cyprus sabotage', *The Wall Street Journal*, 9 October 2007.

49. Among others, (Ambassador) Erato Kozakou-Marcoullis, 'The alleged "isolation" of Turkish Cypriots: Myth and reality', PIO, Republic of Cyprus, 2005; 'The economy of the occupied part of Cyprus: An assessment', Ministry of Finance, Republic of Cyprus, June 2006.

50. Independent scholarship also agrees with some crucial Greek Cypriot arguments; see, among others, Mehmet Ugur, 'EU membership and the north–south development gap in Cyprus: A proposal', in Vassilis K. Fouskas and Heinz A. Richter (eds), *Cyprus and Europe: The Long Way Back*, Mannheim 2003.

51. The Republic claims that the total expenses provided for Turkish Cypriot social insurance pensions and social benefits were £6,760,390 (Cyprus sterling) in 2003, £12,658,297 in 2005 and £15,527,370 in 2006. Whereas between 1975 and 2002 the Republic issued to Turkish Cypriots 4,192 passports, 2,754 ID cards and 4,538 birth certificates, the numbers between 2003 and 2007 soared – obviously because of the Republic's entry to the EU – to 45,488 passports, 74,620 ID cards and 79,898 birth certificates. See, Civil Registry and Migration Department, Republic of Cyprus, 2007 Data.

52. This is tantamount to saying that an Anglo-Saxon plan would have become part and parcel of the French–German historical attempt to politically unify Europe. This is why France has been a firm supporter of the Greek-led Republic of Cyprus throughout. On this, see also Vassilis K. Fouskas, *Zones of Conflict*, London 2003.

53. See, 'Memorandum of Understanding between the Republic of Cyprus and the United Kingdom', 5 June 2008, http://www. number10.gov.uk

54. Ugur, 'EU membership and the north–south development gap in Cyprus'. Ugur's essay was written in 2002 and published in 2003.

55. Robert Solow, 'A contribution to the theory of economic growth', *The Quarterly Journal of Economics*, 70, 1956, pp. 65–94.

56. Paul Samuelson, 'International trade and the equalisation of factor prices', *Economic Journal*, 58, 1948, pp. 163–84.

57. On this topic, see the work by Immanuel Wallerstein, Giovanni Arrighi and others.

58. This adjustment is mediated by diminishing factor returns.

59. Turkish Cypriot authorities argue that they do so because the commodities are imported from a 'third country'. This gives the Greek Cypriots grounds to argue that the motives of the Turkish Cypriots are political: namely, that they use the 'isolation myth' to gain political advantages – see, among others, the speech by the then Republic's Foreign Minister, Yiorgos Lillikas, at the 2006 Cyprus Independence dinner in London on 2 November 2007, http://www.mfa.gov.cy/mfa/mfa2006.nsf

60. David Romer, 'Increasing returns and long-run growth', *The Journal of Political Economy*, 94, 1986, pp. 1002–37.

61. Paul Krugman, *Geography and Trade*, Cambridge (MA) 1991.

62. Turkish Cypriots still have 'personal rights' as EU citizens, but ASA falls outside the scope of EU legislation and fiscal reach.

63. On this theme, cf. Vassilis K. Fouskas, 'The Left and the crisis of the Third Hellenic Republic, 1989–97', in Donald Sassoon (ed.), *Looking Left*, London 1997; James Petras, Evangelos Raptis and Sergio Sarafopoulos, 'Greek socialism: The patrimonial state revisited', in James Kurth and James Petras (eds), *Mediterranean Paradoxes*, Oxford 1993.

64. State Planning Organisation (SPO), Follow Up and Coordination Department, 'Guide for Foreign Investors', Nicosia, February 2007, p. 2. We are grateful to Huseyin Isiksal of Keele University for drawing our attention to the website of SPO (http://www.devplan.org). See also the pages with the main economic and social indicators of ASA, ibid.

65. St. Antony's College, University of Oxford, European Studies Centre, Workshop on Cyprus, 10–11 March 2006.

66. We have compared here SPO data with those of the Statistical Services of the Republic. See also, Nick Kochan, 'Bring Northern Cyprus back into the fold', http://www.msnbc.msn.com/id/21774034/, accessed on 22 November 2007.

67. On these issues, see the comprehensive account by Nikos Skoutaris, 'The application of the *acquis communautaire* in the areas not under the effective control of the Republic of Cyprus: The Green Line regulation', *Common Market Law Review*, 45, 2008, pp. 727–55. The 'Green Line' regulation includes basically provisions on the crossing of persons and goods.

68. Noe and Watson, 'Convergence and reunification of Cyprus: Scope for a virtuous circle', *ECFIN Country Focus*, 2, 2005, pp. 1–6. See also, SPO main social and economic indicators (note 64 above).

69. Robert Barro and Sala-i-Martin, X., *Economic Growth*, New York 1995.

70. Subrata Ghatak and Suha Fethi, 'Economic growth in northern Cyprus: A co-integration analysis, 1977–1996', Economics Discussion Paper/Kingston University Faculty of Human Sciences, London 1999.

71. Ibid., p. 4.

72. See Talat's interview to journalists after meeting the UN Secretary-General Ban Ki-Moon on 17 October 2007.

73. See, 'Easing isolation, Turkish Cypriots to open trade office in Israel', *International Herald Tribune*, 10 March 2008.

74. On this topic, see the perceptive essay by Constantine Tsoukalas, 'European modernity and Greek national identity', *Journal of Southern Europe and the Balkans*, 1, 1999.

75. Bülent Gökay has written wonderful pages on this historical topic. See his PhD dissertation, available from I.B. Tauris (London), *Turkey between the Empires*, 1997.

Bibliography

We have included here only the sources that are cited in the text as it is impossible to list all the material that we have consulted while writing the book

Abramowitz, Morton and Barkey, Henri, 'Cyprus sabotage', *The Wall Street Journal*, 9 October 2007.

Anderson, Perry, 'The divisions of Cyprus', *London Review of Books*, April 2008.

Aybet, Gülnur, 'Turkey's long and winding road to the EU: Implications for the Balkans', *Journal of Southern Europe and the Balkans*, 2006.

Barro, Robert and Sala-i-Martin, Xavier, *Economic Growth*, New York 1995.

Clerides, Glafkos, *My Deposition*, v.3, Nicosia 1997.

Coufoudakis, Van, *Cyprus: A Contemporary Problem in Historical Perspective*, Minnesota 2006.

Coufoudakis, Van, 'Cyprus, the United States and the United Nations since 1960', *Hellenic Studies*, 1994.

Coufoudakis, Van and Kyriakides, Klearchos, *The Case Against the Annan Plan*, London 2004.

Craig, Ian and O'Malley, Brendan, *The Cyprus Conspiracy*, London 1999.

Cyprus Weekly, 5–11 August 2005.

Dekleris, Justice, *The Cyprus Issue 1972–1974: The Last Chance* (in Greek), Athens 1981.

Denktash, Rauf R., *The Cyprus Triangle*, London 1982.

Deutscher, Isaac, 'On the Israeli–Arab war', *New Left Review*, 1967.

Drousiotis, Makarios, *The Dark Side of EOKA* (in Greek), Athens 1999.

Duygun, Meryem Fethi, Sami Fethi and Salih Turan Katircioglu, 'Estimating the size of the Cypriot underground economy: A comparison with European experience', *International Journal of Manpower*, 27, 2006.

Eagleton, Terry, *The Ideology of the Aesthetics*, Oxford 1990.

Emerson, Michael and Tocci, Natalie, *Cyprus as Lighthouse of the East Mediterranean: Shaping Re-unification and EU Accession Together*, Brussels 2002.

European Council – General Affairs Council, 'EU financial support for the Turkish Cypriot community', Brussels, 6810/06 (Presse 60), 27 February 2006.

Evre, Bülent, *Kibris Türk Milliyetçiligi: Oluşumu ve Gelişimi*, Nicosia 2004.

Evriviades, Marios L., 'Review of Claire Palley's...', *Mediterranean Quarterly*, 2006.

Evriviades, Marios L., 'The US and Cyprus: The politics of manipulation in the 1985 UN Cyprus high level meeting', Occasional Research paper no. 3, Institute of International Relations, Athens 1992.

Fouskas, Vassilis K., 'The imprint of Dumbarton Oaks on Cyprus', *Hellenic Studies*, 2004.

Fouskas, Vassilis K., 'The Left and the crisis of the Third Hellenic Republic, 1989–97', in Donald Sassoon (ed.), *Looking Left*, London 1997.

Fouskas, Vassilis K., 'Uncomfortable questions: Cyprus, October 1973–August 1974', *Contemporary European History*, 2005.

Fouskas, Vassilis K., 'US foreign policy in the Greater Middle East during the Cold War and the position of Cyprus', in Vassilis K. Fouskas and Heinz Richter (eds), *Cyprus and Europe: The Long Way Back*, Mannheim 2003.

Fouskas, Vassilis K., *Zones of Conflict: US Foreign Policy in the Balkans and the Greater Middle East*, London 2003.

Fouskas, Vassilis K. and Gökay, Bülent, *The New American Imperialism: Bush's War on Terror and Blood for Oil*, Connecticut 2005.

Frankfurt, Harry G., *On Bullshit*, Princeton 2005.

Ghatak, Subrata and Fethi, Suha, 'Economic growth in Northern Cyprus: A co-integration analysis, 1977–1996', Economics Discussion Paper, Kingston University, London 1999.

Gökay, Bülent, *Turkey between the Empires*, London 1997.

Gowan, Peter, 'UN:US', *New Left Review*, November–December 2003.

Hannay, David, *Cyprus: The Search for a Solution*, London 2005.

Hemming, John, 'North Cyprus: "Tied to motherland"', *Kathimerini* (English edition, insert in *International Herald Tribune*), 9 August 2000.

Hitchens, Christopher, *The Trial of Henry Kissinger*, London 2001.

Holland, Robert, *Britain and the Revolt in Cyprus*, Oxford 1998.

International Crisis Group, Report No. 190, 'Cyprus: Reversing the drift to partition', Brussels, 10 January 2008.

Kitromilides, Paschalis, '"Imagined communities" and the origins of the national question in the Balkans', in M. Blinkhorn (ed.), *Modern Greece: Nationalism and Nationality*, London 1990.

Kitromilides, Paschalis, 'Tradition, Enlightenment and Revolution', PhD dissertation, Harvard University 1978.

Kizilyrek, Niyazi, *The Deadlock of Nationalisms* (in Greek), Athens 1999.

Kochan, Nick, 'Bring Northern Cyprus back into the fold', http://www.ft.com, accessed on 22 November 2007.

Kolko, Gabriel, *The Politics of War*, New York 1968.

Krugman, Paul, *Geography and Trade*, Cambridge (MA) 1991.

Kyriakou, Andreas P., *A Viable Solution to the Cyprus Problem: Lessons from Political Economy*, Nicosia 2003.

Lasswell, Harold, *Essays on the Garrison State*, New Brunswick 1997.

Lijphart, Arend, *Democracies: Patterns of Majoritarian and Consensus Government in Twenty-one Countries*, New Haven 1984.

Lillikas, Yiorghos, Cyprus Independence Dinner in London 2006, www.mfa.gov.cy

Marcoulis-Kozakou, Erato, 'The alleged "isolation" of Turkish Cypriots: Myth and reality', PIO, Republic of Cyprus, 2005.

Makovsky, Alan, 'Turkey's faded European dream', paper presented to the Conference 'The Parameters of partnership: Germany, the US and Turkey', American Institute for Contemporary German Studies, The Johns Hopkins University, Washington DC 1997.

Mallinson, William, *Cyprus: A Modern History*, London 2005 (reprinted in paperback in 2008).

Markides, Weston Diana, *Cyprus 1957–63: From Colonial Conflict to Constitutional Crisis. The Key Role of the Municipal Issue*, Minnesota 2001.

'Memorandum of Understanding between the Republic of Cyprus and the United Kingdom', 5 June 2008.

Ministry of Finance, 'The economy of the occupied part of Cyprus: An assessment', Republic of Cyprus, June 2006.

Moran, Michael (ed.), *Rauf Denktash at the United Nations: Speeches on Cyprus*, Cambridge 1997.

Necatigil, Zaim M., *The Cyprus Question and the Turkish Position in International Law*, Oxford 1996.

Nicolet, Claude, *United States Policy Towards Cyprus, 1954–1974*, Mannheim 2001.

Packard, Martin, *Getting it Wrong: Fragments from a Cyprus Diary*, Milton Keynes 2008.

Palley, Claire, *An International Relations Debacle: The UN Secretary-General's Mission of Good Offices in Cyprus, 1999–2004*, Oxford 2005.

Petras, James et al. (eds), *Mediterranean Paradoxes*, Oxford 1993.

Reports of the UN Secretary-General on UN Operations in Cyprus, S/2004/437, S/2006/931, S/2007/699.

Romer, David, 'Increasing Returns and Long-Run Growth', *The Journal of Political Economy*, 94, 1986.

Samuelson, Peter, 'International trade and the equalisation of factor prices', *Economic Journal*, 58, 1948.

Sarris, Neoklis, *The Other Side* (in Greek), Athens, many editions.

Skoutaris, Nikos, 'The application of the *acquis communautaire* in the areas not under the effective control of the Republic of Cyprus: The Green Line regulation', *Common Market Law Review*, 45, 2008.

Slaughter, Matthew J., 'Per capita income convergence and the role of international trade', *American Economic Review*, 87, No. 2.

Solow, Robert, 'A contribution to the theory of economic growth', *The Quarterly Journal of Economics*, 70, 1956.

St. Antony's College, University of Oxford, European Studies Centre, *Workshop on Cyprus*, 10–11 March 2006.

State Planning Organisation (Areas of Suspended Acquis), 'Guide for Investors', Nicosia 2007.

Stefanides, Ioannis, *Isle of Discord*, London 1999.

Talat, Ali Mehmet, 'Turkish Cypriots' expectations from the EU', *Turkish Policy Quarterly*, Fall 2005.

Tsoukalas, Constantine, 'European modernity and Greek national identity', *Journal of Southern Europe and the Balkans*, 1, 1999.

Ugur, Mehmet, 'EU membership and the North–South development gap in Cyprus: A proposal', in Vassilis K. Fouskas and Heinz Richter (eds), *Cyprus and Europe: The Long Way Back*, Mannheim 2003.

Unsigned, 'Easing isolation, Turkish Cypriots to open trade office in Israel', *International Herald Tribune*, 10 March 2008.

Index

Compiled by Sue Carlton

Page numbers followed by n refer to the endnotes